POCKET HOLE
JOINERY

**Bookshelf · Daybed · Mirror/picture frame
Dresser · Bathroom vanity...AND MORE!**

MARK EDMUNDSON

The Taunton Press
Inspiration for hands-on living®

The Taunton Press
Inspiration for hands-on living®

The Taunton Press, Inc.,
63 South Main Street, PO Box 5506, Newtown, CT 06470-5506
e-mail: tp@taunton.com

Editor: Peter Chapman
Copy Editor: Diane Sinitsky
Interior Design/Layout: Tinsley Morrison
Photographer: All photos by Mark Edmundson, except pp. 2, 3, 14, 29, 46, 61, 77, 98, 153
by David Marx Photography; p. 6 (middle photo) © Kreg Tool Company
Illustrator: Mario Ferro

The following manufacturers/names appearing in *Pocket Hole Joinery* are trademarks: Blum®, Daly's® ProFin™,
Deft®, Dowelmax®, JessEm™, Kreg®, Masonite®, Porter-Cable®, Rockler® Pock-it Hole Clamp®, Watco®.

Library of Congress Cataloging-in-Publication Data in progress

ISBN 978-1-62113-674-3

Printed in the United States of America
10 9 8 7 6 5 4 3 2 1

ABOUT YOUR SAFETY

Working wood is inherently dangerous. Using hand or power tools improperly or ignoring safety practices
can lead to permanent injury or even death. Don't try to perform operations you learn about here (or else-
where) unless you're certain they are safe for you. If something about an operation doesn't feel right, don't
do it. Look for another way. We want you to enjoy the craft, so please keep safety foremost in your mind
whenever you're in the shop.

Acknowledgments

I'd like to thank my wife, Jill, for allowing me to explore my woodworking passion all these years. I'd also like to acknowledge Asa Christiana and Tom McKenna at The Taunton Press for keeping me in the writing loop with tool reviews and articles, and the College of the Redwoods Fine Woodworking program, which shaped me as a builder and provided me the chance to push myself beyond what I ever thought possible.

Contents

Introduction

I attended the College of the Redwoods Fine Woodworking program from 1995 to 1997. While enrolled, I learned how to perform some of the most challenging ways of constructing furniture possible, including curved surfaces, shop-sawn veneer, and hand-cut dovetails. Among other things, we strived for drawers that closed on a cushion of air. Projects could be so complex that it was helpful to build a mock-up of the piece beforehand to see how it looked full size and make tweaks to the design. The mock-up was usually made with cardboard and scrapwood using tape,

hot glue, and face screwing to hold the pieces together long enough to make sure the design warranted the long hours it would take to construct.

During my second year, I saw another student secretly use a Kreg® pocket hole jig to construct his mock-up. He kept it hidden at his bench and never used it in view of any of the teachers. Even though they were mock-ups we were building, I would always get distracted by the screws and tape used to hold it together. Plus, the mock-ups were constantly falling apart and it would get frustrating. So one evening I borrowed

my fellow student's jig. I was impressed with how easy it was to use and how strong the joint appeared to be and that the mock-up wouldn't fall apart in a day.

After finishing the program, my first project was a basic kitchen. With limited tools at that time, I knew the pocket hole jig would come in handy and I purchased one for the job. At first, I didn't use it to its full potential but only in weird situations where I needed a piece of wood to be attached to another piece of wood but couldn't get in a position to nail or face-screw it. Later, as I started to build kitchen cabinets that required face frames, it really started to show me its potential.

Although at this time I was trying to get jobs building custom pieces, friends or acquaintances would always ask about my work. Their budgets weren't nearly as large as some of my clients, but they liked my work and I wanted to help them out. My first full pocket-screwed piece of furniture was for my bike mechanic. We were doing a trade and my work time was limited, so I just exchanged the mortise-and-tenon joinery for pocket screws. It was an entryway table with drawers and by all appearances looked the same as if I'd used traditional techniques. Pocket screws became my go-to option for projects for people with limited budgets. I could still design it the same, use nice wood and a smooth finish, but avoid the time-consuming joinery details. The main thing was when the piece was done, I could look at it and be proud of my work and know that clients would be really happy with it.

Now I use pocket screws not only for furniture for my friends on limited budgets but for a whole range of custom projects as well. It's a quick, easy, and efficient way to build furniture, as you'll see in the eight projects that follow.

1 POCKET HOLE JOINERY BASICS

At its most basic, pocket hole joinery boils down to a game of "hide the screw." The object is to join two pieces of wood either at a right angle or parallel to each other. Screws are driven through predrilled holes into the mating piece of wood so that the joint is tight and the screws are hidden from view. A tight joint garners the most points, and a well-hidden screw comes in second. Building a jig out of pocket screws that helps perform the main pocket hole joinery task gets you extra points. Having to use pocket hole plugs to cover your tracks should only be considered as a last resort and does not count toward the point total.

But, of course, it's about more than just playing a game and having some fun. Pocket hole joinery provides a real advantage for beginning woodworkers and veterans alike. The first benefit is its relatively low cost for the tooling, with the most basic jig and clamp set costing less than $75. Second, pocket hole joinery is easy to learn. There are some skills required, but if you can pull the trigger on a drill and place a clamp, you can start joining wood with pocket screws. The third advantage is speed. Pieces go together so

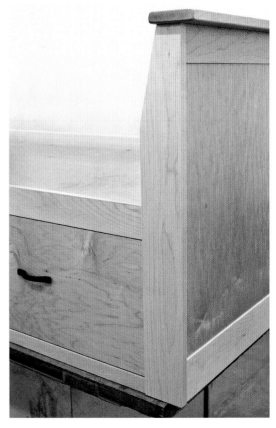

With pocket hole joinery, you can create strong joints without a single screw or screw hole visible. This is a detail of the daybed project (see p. 77).

Attaching edge-banding to a board (here, a corner shelf) is a common and easy application for pocket hole joinery.

quickly that it will redefine what you're able to build within a limited time. But low cost, ease of use, and speed would not be enough to justify its use unless the joints created were also strong. Luckily, pocket hole joinery has that covered, too. A pocket hole joint won't come apart without a good deal of force . . . and without taking a fair amount of wood with it.

WORK SMART

The strength of screwing pocket holes compared with face screwing is that the screws are not driven into end grain, which is prone to split and strip out. The screws come from the end grain and go into side grain, giving the screws plenty to grab on to. It's basically a toe-nailed screw.

Pocket Hole Applications

To illustrate the advantage of pocket hole joinery, imagine attaching a solid edge-band to a flat plywood surface. Your options in lieu of pocket screws are finish nailing, face screwing, or biscuits and glue. A finish nail is the most often used and leaves a small hole that is easily filled with putty. It's not the strongest joint, usually leaves a small gap somewhere along the line, requires a compressor and nail gun, and does leave behind the putty hole. Face screwing is simple and strong, requires only a drill gun, but also requires a plug that will need to be sanded flush or a lot of putty to cover the hole. The screws are prone to stripping out or causing the plywood to delaminate since they are driven into the core. It's most definitely not hidden from view.

Using biscuits and glue is a strong option but requires a biscuit jointer and time to let the glue set up. It also requires a few more steps to mark the mating location of the biscuits and to cut slots in both the panel and edge-band. Biscuit joinery doesn't leave behind holes that need to be plugged, so it's a step in the right direction.

A pocket hole will easily join the edge-banding to the plywood panel, without the need for putty or sanding a plug flush. It can be completely hidden from view. The holes in the panel can be drilled very quickly. And if the joint is to be glued, there is no need to wait for the glue to dry to continue working.

Edge-banding is one of the many applications of pocket screws. The obvious use for pocket hole joinery is in the construction of face frames. Since the back of a face frame is usually hidden from view, it's easy to lay out the pocket hole locations. The other options of using dowels, loose tenons, or machine-cut mortises and tenons will almost always be more time-consuming, require more expensive tools, and be more difficult to assemble because glue will need to dry and the clamping can get a bit technical. Essentially, pocket hole joinery can be used in any instance where you can hide the screw.

Situations that are not as advantageous are those where the screw cannot be hidden from view and require the pocket hole to be plugged. It's not that the plugs don't do the job, but it kind of ends up a zero-sum game. Plugs have come in handy for me where I really wanted to use pocket screws but also did not want a glaring hole that would be visible and accumulate debris—under a sink, for example. But gluing and flush-sanding the plugs is more difficult and time-consuming than you'd imagine. They don't pair very well, and the fit is not exactly tight. Fortunately, I rarely need to use them since there always seems to be a way to hide the screw.

Pocket Hole Jigs

There are several pocket hole jigs available for purchase, from inexpensive portable models to larger, more expensive benchtop machines with built-in drill motors. I originally started out with the basic cast-aluminum Kreg jig. This jig only drills holes for 1¼-in. screws mainly through ¾-in. stock. At first I avoided purchasing the face clamp and used C-clamps instead. The face clamp seemed like an added expense that wouldn't be that much better than using clamps. When I finally did purchase a face clamp, I was astounded by how much easier it was to use and felt like I had wasted time in my attempt to save some money.

I eventually purchased the Kreg Jig K3 Master System. Although more options sometimes lead to more problems, like forgetting to

Shown clockwise from left, the benchtop Kreg Jig K3 (featured throughout this book), a portable jig base, and the small Kreg Jig R3.

The Kreg Jig K4 Master System includes a benchtop jig and all the accessories necessary for pocket hole joinery.

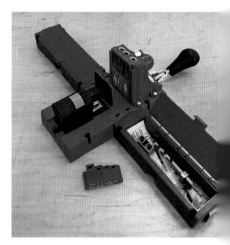

The Kreg Jig K5, an updated version of the K3, has a front-mounted clamp handle that makes clamping easy.

Choosing a Jig

If you're buying your first pocket hole jig, my advice is to go with the Kreg Jig K4 Master System (see the middle photo on the facing page). This jig will cover all the bases and includes the face clamp and portable clamping jig, which is a definite plus. It will provide you with the tools necessary to build all the projects in this book.

The Kreg Jig K5 is the latest offering from Kreg (right photo on the facing page). It has a clamp that is accessed from the drill side of the jig and a ratcheting clamp mechanism that can adjust to different stock thicknesses without tools. The advantage of the K5 is that you don't have to reach over the work to access the clamp, which can get tiring on large plywood panels. While the K5 costs less than the Master System, it does not include the face clamp or the portable clamping jig. Both of these items can be purchased separately, which would make it a great system when complete.

Drilling goes quickly with the Porter-Cable QuikJig, and a handy scale on the side tells you the screw length you need for your setup.

reset the jig for ³/₄-in. thickness and drilling holes too deep, overall the versatility won out over my original jig. Being able to go from portable to benchtop so easily is a great option that speeds up work. My benchtop Kreg Foreman (see the photo on p. 49) is a more expensive machine, but it's worth the money to me as it is so easy to use and is always at the ready. If I have a large stack of cabinet parts that need to be drilled, I can do the job quickly with less effort. The most affordable Kreg jig (the R3) is very small but still does the job. It has the advantage of being able to drill a pocket hole in locations where clamps can't be used. Although the occasions are rare, when I do need it, it's the only tool for the job.

A few years ago Porter-Cable® came out with the QuikJig, a full redesign of its pocket hole jig.

When I had the opportunity to use the jig on a job, I was impressed by its sturdy construction and self-adjusting thickness clamps, which set it apart from other jigs I've used. What didn't work for me was the need to have a large assortment of screw sizes at the ready. Since the jig automatically adjusts the screw depth based on the stock thickness, it's not possible to drill out a 1¹/₂-in.-thick piece to use a 1¹/₄-in. screw. I rarely use screws longer than 1¹/₄ in., even if I'm drilling stock thicker than ³/₄ in. It just doesn't seem as important to increase screw length to coincide with stock thickness. That being said, the Porter-Cable is a fine jig that is easy to use, and if switching between stock of varying thickness is something you find yourself doing often, the Porter-Cable will be a great value.

Sled for Jig

Building a platform for the pocket hole jig to attach to helps to support the pieces being drilled and makes clamping the jig to a benchtop a snap. My sled is simply a 9¼-in. by 39-in. piece of ¾-in. plywood with a strip of ¼-in. and ¾-in. stock that equals the height of the jig on either side to help support long pieces.

DRILLS

To go along with the jig, you'll need a drill. This can simply be a screw gun that alternates between drill mode for drilling the pocket hole and screw mode for driving the screw. Now that impact drivers are more affordable, the options have increased. Impact drivers work really well to drive pocket screws except for one thing: They are loud, which makes it hard to hear when the screw is close to being set. With a screw gun, you can tell when the screw is seated because the motor will slow down. With an impact driver, the motor slowdown is subtler and actually requires looking at the driver to see the change in speed. It takes a while to get used to using an impact driver, but it's the tool I use most often for driving pocket screws.

DRILL BITS, DRIVERS, AND POCKET SCREWS

In addition to the stepped drill bit that comes with the jig, an extra-long ⅛-in. drill bit comes in handy for predrilling. These bits are available from most hardware stores and help when you want to get the hole started or are worried about the potential for splitting. Driver bits are also necessary. The long 6-in. driver is my go-to,

An impact driver is the best tool to use to install pocket screws.

but having a shorter 3-in. driver is helpful for tighter spots.

Pocket screws come in coarse and fine thread. To keep things simple, I just keep the fine-thread 1¼-in. screws in stock and don't usually switch between coarse and fine as the wood type changes (though for very soft woods, the coarse thread is better). On occasion, I use standard decking screws, making sure not to over-torque to avoid splitting around the pocket hole.

CLAMPS

Clamps are also mandatory. For starters, make sure to purchase at least the 3-in. throat vice (face) clamp. There are a lot of pocket screw–specific clamps available; while they can be useful on occasion, none of the many I have used have stood out as a necessity as much as the face clamp. A lightweight set of aluminum 36-in. bar clamps will come in handy, too.

RIGHT-ANGLE JIG

To help with clamping, a simple right-angle jig constructed from two pieces of ¾-in. scrapwood is invaluable (see the photo on p. 10). The boards for mine are 4½ in. by 12 in. Drill two pocket holes on one end of one of the boards and join the two in a right angle. Attach a right triangle of ¼-in. plywood to make it square. The jig can be clamped to pieces to help hold them upright during assembly.

Problems and Solutions

To say that pocket hole joinery is the answer to all your dreams for furniture making would be a disservice to anyone looking to utilize pocket screws. In this section, I'll lay out some of the frustrating aspects of pocket hole joinery and offer some possible solutions.

THE PROBLEM OF SHIFT

The complaint most often heard with pocket hole joinery is that a shift occurs when joining

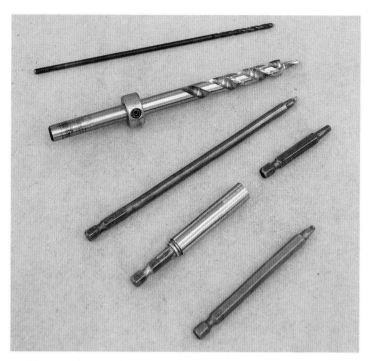

Drill bits and drivers, from the top: a ⅛-in. extra-long predrill bit; a ⅜-in. stepped pocket hole drill bit; a 6-in. square driver; a 2-in. square driver and extension; and a 3-in. square driver.

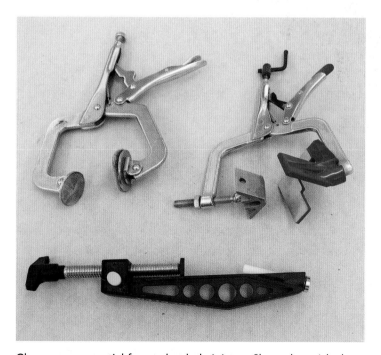

Clamps are essential for pocket hole joinery. Shown here (clockwise from top) are a face clamp, a 90-degree corner clamp, and a Rockler® Pock-it Hole Clamp® with Quick Release.

A right-angle jig clamped to the workpiece (and bench) helps to hold the piece upright during assembly.

To Glue or Not to Glue?

Glue should be used whenever it's mandatory that a joint not shift at all after assembly. An example of this would be a flush butt joint. The glue isn't used so much for strength—the screws provide plenty of that—but instead to make sure that small incremental shifts do not happen that would create a ridge, usually only noticeable by touch.

It's surprising to many people how little I use glue with pocket screws. One reason is that my joints are often between stock of different thicknesses. This step is a common detail in Craftsman style, which is apparent in my designs. A small incremental shift during assembly of the joint will not be noticeable if the stock is already stepped. If glue is necessary for strength, then the design may be flawed. A dab of glue on the end grain of a piece of wood does not provide a significant increase in strength of the joint.

two pieces of wood so that the alignment does not come out as expected. Why does this shift occur? The obvious answer is that the screw pulls in the direction that it is driving, but there is more going on than that. If you've ever tried to drill a hole off 90 degrees to a surface, you know the tendency for the drill bit to walk in the direction it's pointing. The tip of that pocket screw with its self-tapping auger point acts like a drill bit so that the force on the screw tip is pushing it in the direction that it's screwing.

Next, there is the stepped drill hole. For starters, the threaded tip of the screw must be able to slide easily into the predrilled hole so the size of the small tip on the drill bit is as wide as the threaded section of the screw. It's a nice fit between the two, not too sloppy but loose enough that the screw can be seated in the hole without much effort. But the width of the shank without threads ends up being narrower than the predrilled hole, so there is a bit of wiggle room around the unthreaded screw shaft.

Here, you can see the gap around the unthreaded shaft and the small plug of wood at the tip of the screw before it is driven.

You'll notice that the threaded section of the screw occurs in both the pocket hole portion and in the wood being joined.

As a result, there is just enough room for the attaching piece of wood to shift around the screw shank.

Notice that the predrilled hole does not go all the way through but stops about 1/16 in. from breaking through the end-grain surface. This last little piece of wood is important. It serves as a plug around the tip of the threads to help ensure that when the tip transfers from the vertical piece into the mating piece there is less chance of wandering. When the screw passes through different layers of wood is when the opportunity for shift occurs.

MINIMIZING SHIFT

We know the mechanics of pocket screw joinery has a tendency to pull the pieces in the direction of the screw, so how do you minimize this? Typically, clamping is the easiest cure. Using either the face clamp or bar clamps to hold the pieces tight while screwing will greatly reduce shift.

Sometimes, though, it's difficult to get good clamping pressure. In these cases, preventative

Commercial ¾-in. plywood (left) is often less thick than ¾-in. solid stock (right), which can pose the risk of the screw tip breaching the surface.

The pocket holes on the left were predrilled ⅛ in. deep to minimize shift. The pocket holes on the right were predrilled ⅜ in. deep to minimize stress.

A deep ⅜-in. predrill still leaves just enough material for the threads to bite.

measures are needed. The first and easiest is to expect shift and thus clamp in a way that offsets the anticipated outcome. If the shift doesn't happen but you compensated for it, simply tap the piece until it's flush. It's very easy to tap in the direction of the screw. It is nearly impossible to tap against the direction of the screw without having it bounce back.

Another technique is to predrill ⅛ in. deep between the two pieces being joined with an extra-long ⅛-in. drill bit. What this does is start the hole so that the tip doesn't have the tendency to walk when passing through the joint surfaces. This can also help eliminate splitting of narrow pieces.

SPLITTING

Splitting is another situation to watch out for. The combination of the predrilled stepped hole and self-tapping screws does a great job, but splitting, especially on narrow stock, is a possi-

bility. It seems to happen when the grain is either knotty or of a density different from the rest of the area. One problem I ran into was when edge-joining two pieces of hickory. The screw landed directly across from a tight knot that I didn't notice, so when I drove the screw, the area through the knot cracked. For that reason, it's a good idea to take note of knotty or especially dense areas and avoid them or use a predrill bit drilling ¼ in. or ⅜ in. deep to reduce the pressure around the screw.

BROKEN SCREWS

Dense wood or knotty areas can also cause screws to break. If the wood is very dense like maple or oak, make sure not to over-torque the screws or they will snap. This usually occurs when you're trying to get a small gap to close that isn't clamped and the extra turn is too much. With softwoods like alder and pine, the screws just keep going. This can pose another problem of the screw tip breaching the surface, especially when using an impact screw gun or on commercial ¾-in. plywood, which is often less than a ¾ in. thick.

END-GRAIN POPOUT

Sometimes on the pocket-drilled end grain there will be a little fleck of wood at the tip of the predrilled hole that has come unseated during drilling. Should you pick it out or pound it back in? I choose to pound it back in to help secure the plug that I mentioned earlier. You might also want to check the stop collar on the drill bit to make sure it's not set too deep.

Prefinishing

With most of the projects in this book, I chose to prefinish the pieces before assembly. I feel the end result outweighs the precautions that need to be taken. It also might be a case of which came first: the chicken or the egg. Do I prefinish because pocket hole joinery makes it so easy, or do I use pocket hole joinery because it works so well in conjunction with prefinishing?

As mentioned in the glue sidebar on p. 10, I usually join stock that has a small step between surfaces. I like this detail, which is often used in the Craftsman-style furniture that provides most of my inspiration. This offset hides any shift that might occur when screwing and eliminates the need for flush-sanding and gluing since a small shift will not be noticeable. Applying finish into those small steps is a bit tricky, so I usually finish before assembly. It's easier to sand between coats and to apply the oil in nice even passes along the entire length of the piece. The difficulty in prefinishing is that you must take great care not to scratch or ding the work during assembly. That means protective leather cauls on all the clamps and protective blankets on work surfaces. Once you get used to these extra steps, the payback is worth it. At a minimum,

applying one or two coats to the pieces before assembly and finishing with two more additional coats after it is assembled would still bring you out ahead.

End-grain popout occurs when a little piece of wood at the tip of a predrilled hole comes unseated.

2 BLANKET BENCH

The tops of benches always seem to accumulate stuff, so adding a shelf below this blanket bench should help to alleviate that problem. Adding the shelf also hides some pocket holes, so it's a win-win as far as furniture details go. The benchtop planks are the biggest pieces required at 5¾ in. wide and 38 in. long, but the rest of the pieces are either narrow or short. The machining is basic, and it's possible to build this bench with just a tablesaw, jigsaw, and pocket screw jig. A chopsaw or sliding crosscut sled to cut multiple parts to the same length would be helpful to ensure tight joints but is not essential. Overall, this is a very simple project for the beginning woodworker that illustrates how versatile pocket hole joinery can be.

MATERIALS

QUANTITY	PART	ACTUAL SIZE	CONSTRUCTION NOTES
4	Bench ends	¾ in. × 5¾ in. × 17¼ in.	Black walnut
2	Benchtop	¾ in. × 5¾ in. × 38 in.	Black walnut
2	Benchtop center strips	¾ in. × 1½ in. × 16¾ in.	Black walnut
4	Shelf slats	¾ in. × 2¾ in. × 32 in.	Alder
2	Skirts	¾ in. × 2¾ in. × 32 in.	Alder

Stock Preparation

All the material on the bench is ¾ in. thick. You can mill your own boards, of course, but it's easier to purchase S4S ("surfaced four sides") planks from the lumberyard and avoid joining and planing. The wide widths are all 5¾ in., the skirt and lower slats are 2¾ in., and the narrow strips on the top are 1½ in. wide. This project requires no glue, biscuits, or dowels—just pocket screws. To further simplify construction, I used only the right-angle jig, two face clamps, and a couple of small bar clamps for assembly.

There are several ways to spice up this bench. I used contrasting wood for the skirt and lower shelf; other combinations might be matching wood for the top and shelf and a different wood for the ends and skirts. Cut all the parts to length, but note that the lower shelf stock and skirts will initially be cut at 32 in. and then later trimmed to 31½ in. Label which faces will

WORK SMART

When labeling parts, try to mark in an area that will not be visible after the bench is assembled, such as the end grain on the ends and the underside of the benchtop.

be out, front, back, right, and left on all the parts, and then sand away the machine marks on the surfaces that will be visible. To make edge-joining the ends, lower shelf, and benchtop easier, bevel the corners at the edge joints with a block plane or sanding pad first, which negates the need to sand the joint flush after pocket screwing.

Assembling the Bench Ends

The bench ends, which are made up of two 5¾-in. by 17¼-in. pieces, get two sets of pocket holes. The first group of four holes joins the two end boards together. On the back 5¾-in. boards, measure down from the top along the inside edge ¾ in. and 2¼ in., and mark for the top pocket screws (see the drawing on p. 17). From the bottom, measure up 2½ in. and 3½ in., and mark for the bottom set of pocket screws. The next group of holes attaches the bench ends to the benchtop and is located along the top inside edge. Measure over 1¼ in. from both edges on the inside face on all four boards, and mark for the pocket hole. Drill the pocket holes in the end stock.

Use the right-angle jig to hold the front 5¾-in. end piece with the center edge up and the inside facing out. Place the back end piece

(Continued on p. 19)

Drill the pocket holes in the four bench-end pieces. Building a sled for your pocket hole jig (see p. 8) helps support the stock and allows the jig to be clamped to your work surface.

Clamp the right-angle jig to the end piece to help hold it upright during assembly.

Center a face clamp over the seam between the end pieces as you drive the pocket screws.

Use a roll of tape to help draw the curve in the bottom edge of the bench end.

BENCH END AND SKIRT DETAIL

Skirt detail

⅞ in.

2¾ in.

2¼ in.

4 in.

3 in.

¼ in.

Skirt

4 in.

15¾ in.

27½ in.

2¾ in.

31½ in.

Bench end

1¼ in.

1¼ in.

5¾ in.

Back

17¼ in.

¾ in.

2¼ in.

1 in.

2½ in.

3½ in.

2½ in.

WORK SMART

The exact location of the pocket holes isn't supercritical. The measurements are intended to keep screws from colliding and from being hard to reach during assembly. Once you get good at using pocket screws, you'll be able to lay out their location by eye without measuring.

BENCHTOP AND LOWER SHELF

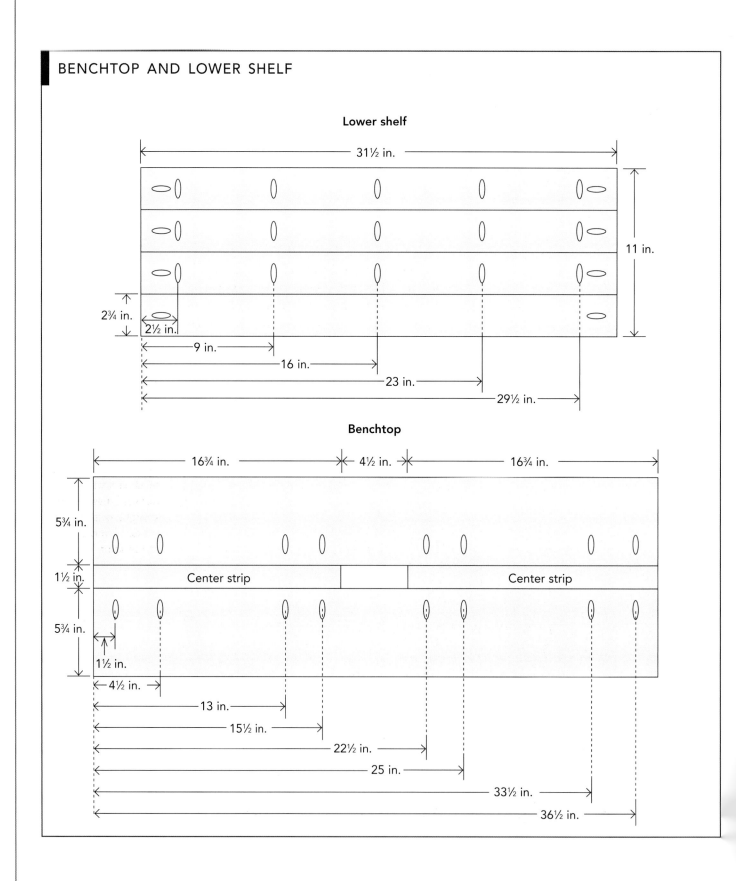

Lower shelf

31½ in.

11 in.

2¾ in.

2½ in.

9 in.

16 in.

23 in.

29½ in.

Benchtop

16¾ in.

4½ in.

16¾ in.

5¾ in.

1½ in.

Center strip

Center strip

5¾ in.

1½ in.

4½ in.

13 in.

15½ in.

22½ in.

25 in.

33½ in.

36½ in.

on top, flush up the top edge, and hold with the face clamp. Drive two pocket screws into the top pair of holes. Then move the right-angle jig to the top edge and repeat for the bottom pair of holes. Assemble the opposite end in the same manner.

Curves cut into the bottom edge of each bench end are a subtle design touch (and echo the curves cut in the skirt). Measure in 2½ in. from each side and make a mark on the bottom edge. Using a try square, draw a line 1 in. up from the bottom edge between the 2½-in. marks. Use a roll of tape or similar rounded object to trace the curve between the 2½-in. mark and the 1-in. line. Cut out the curves and clean up the edges with a file or sander.

Assembling the Lower Shelf

Three of the four 2¾-in. lower shelf slats receive pocket holes for assembly (the front slat

The right-angle jig is really helpful when assembling the bench; if you haven't already built one (see p. 8), I suggest you take a minute to do so now.

does not get drilled for assembly, but it will get drilled at either end after the shelf is cut to length). Make marks on the underside of the #2, #3, and #4 slats at 2½ in., 9 in., 16 in., 23 in., and 29½ in. (see the drawing on the facing page). Drill pocket holes at the marks. Next, take the front slat (the one without any pocket holes) and clamp it to the right-angle jig so that the bottom faces out. Place the #2 slat on top of the front slat, flush up the end, and hold tight with the face clamp at the opposite end of the

Mark the #2, #3, and #4 shelf slats for pocket holes, using a straightedge to mark across all three slats at the same time.

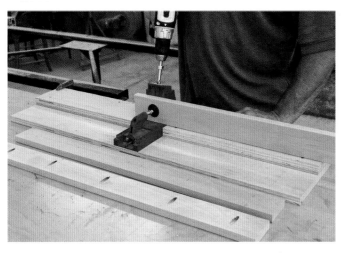

Use the marks on the slats to align them on the jig for drilling.

Starting at the opposite end from the right-angle jig, clamp the slats and drive the first screw.

WORK SMART

Always clamp if you can. Although it may be tempting not to clamp every pocket hole during assembly, it's a good habit to get into—especially if it's important that the pieces don't shift.

Continue adding the shelf slats until all four are in place.

Wait until all of the slats have been assembled, then move the right-angle jig to the center and drive the last screw on each slat.

right-angle jig. The ends don't need to be perfect since the shelf will be cut to 31 1/2 in. after it is assembled. Starting at the end, drive a pocket screw and then move the clamp to the next hole and repeat. Do not drive the last pocket screw located in front of the right-angle jig yet. Set the #3 slat on top and repeat the drilling procedure, then set the #4 slat on top and repeat. Move the right-angle jig to the middle, and drive the pocket holes that were skipped at the end.

Assembling the Benchtop

The benchtop is composed of two 5 3/4-in. by 38-in. planks and two 1 1/2-in. by 16 3/4-in. center strips, all of which are 3/4 in. thick. The space between the center strips not only provides a handhold for carrying the bench but also allows you to slip the face clamp in between the slats to hold it tight when driving the center pocket screws. The pocket holes, located on the two 38-in. planks, must be within reach of the face clamps so the holes can be secured during assembly and not interfere with the pocket screws on the ends that attach the top. On the underside of the 38-in. boards, mark for pocket holes on the inside edge at 1 1/2 in., 4 1/2 in., 13 in., 15 1/2 in., 22 1/2 in., 25 in., 33 1/2 in., and 36 1/2 in. Drill out all the pocket holes.

Clamp the back 5 3/4-in. board to the right-angle jig at one end. To reach the holes with the drill, the surface must be close to the edge of the workbench; otherwise, the edge of the bench will get in the way of the drill. Place the 1 1/2-in. center strip on top of the 5 3/4-in. board, flushing up the end. Set the face clamp over the second, 4 1/2-in. pocket hole and drive a screw. Continue down the edge, securing the first strip. Then attach the second strip, again flushing up the end. There should be a 4 1/2-in. gap between the two strips. Attach the second strip with pocket screws, using the face clamp to hold it secure.

Clamp the back benchtop board to the right-angle jig, and set one of the center strips on top. Hold firm with the face clamp while you drill the second pocket screw from the end.

Place the front board on top of the center strips, set the face clamp over the first hole, and drive a pocket screw.

Slide the face clamp in between the gap in the strips, position it over the hole, and drive the screw.

Next, place the front 5¾-in. board on top of the strips. At the opposite end of the right-angle jig, hold tight with the face clamp and drive the first pair of screws. Slip the face clamp in between the gap between the strips and drive screws into the next pair of holes. Reposition the clamp onto the other strip and drive the screws. Remove the face clamp and slide the right-angle jig to the opposite end. Clamp and drive the screws that were located in front of the right-angle jig.

Prepping the Shelf and Skirt

The lower shelf and skirt material need to be cut to 31½ in. to ensure that the ends of the shelf meet squarely with the bench ends. Set a stop block to cut the shelf at 31¾ in. After this first cut, set the stop block to cut the shelf at 31½ in. and trim the other end of the shelf. Cut the skirt material at the same time to 31½ in.

On the underneath side of the shelf are four pocket holes on either end located in the center of each 2¾-in. shelf slat; drill these now. On the inside face of the skirts, drill pocket holes at both ends. Measure down from the top edge

Drill one pocket hole at each end of each slat to attach the shelf to the bench ends.

Use a square to mark the 45-degree start of the curve on the lower edge of the skirt.

Gently draw the curve created by the batten onto the skirt.

$^7/_8$ in. and $2^1/_4$ in. and mark for pocket holes. Along the top inside edge of the skirts are three pocket holes to attach the skirt to the top. Measure over 4 in., $15^3/_4$ in., and $27^1/_2$ in., and mark for the pocket holes.

The skirts have a gentle curve on the bottom edge that needs to be laid out and cut. Starting with one of the skirts, measure over 3 in. on both ends, and draw a 45-degree mark at least $^1/_2$ in. long. With a square, mark the point at which the 45-degree mark is $^1/_4$ in. above the bottom edge. At the center of the skirt, make a mark $^1/_2$ in. up from the bottom edge. Clamp a small scrap of wood at that $^1/_2$-in. mark. Take a strip of knot-free wood, $^1/_8$ in. thick or so, and place it on top of the skirt behind the small piece of wood. Since the narrow strip would be hard to clamp, hold it in place with a tape measure or similar weighted object, and force one end of the strip over the $^1/_4$-in. and 45-degree intersections. Do the same thing at the opposite end. Lightly trace the curve, being careful not to push the batten strip out of fair. Cut the curve and round over the edges with a file and sanding block on both stretchers. Repeat for the second skirt.

WORK
SMART

If you have a scrap of smooth plywood similar in size to the benchtop, lay it on a pair of sawhorses. In this manner, you'll be able to clamp from both sides without turning the bench around as you would if you built it on a wide table.

Assembling the Bench

Set the benchtop face down on the work surface. The benchtop overhangs the base ends by $2^1/_2$ in. on either side. To help locate the bench end, clamp a $2^1/_2$-in.-wide scrap of wood to the end of the top so that the edges are flush. Check with a square, and shift the scrap so that it is

Square up the scrap spacer with the front edge of the bench.

Mark the center of the benchtop in front of the spacer to help align the bench ends.

Mark the edge of the bench end, which should be ¾ in. from the front edge of the top.

square with the front edge. With a tape measure, mark the center of the bench in front of the 2½-in. spacer. Place the end piece so that the center joint is directly above the center mark on the bench. Mark the front edge of the bench end where it meets the benchtop (¾ in. in from the front edge of the top).

Clamp the right-angle jig to the inside of the bench end and then to the benchtop. Drive the first pocket screw in the end and then remove the right-angle jig and drive the remaining screws into the benchtop. The end should be tight against the 2½-in. spacer when driving the screws. Remove the 2½-in. spacer.

The skirt steps in from the front edge of the top 1 in. To help locate the skirt, rip a 1-in. strip of wood on the tablesaw and then clamp it flush with the front edge of the top. Slide the skirt into place and clamp it to the bench (see the top photo on p. 26). Set both screws into the bench end, driving the pocket hole closest to the benchtop first. Then drive the end screw from the skirt into the benchtop. Move the 1-in. spacer in front of the center pocket hole in the skirt and drive the screw into the benchtop, then move the spacer down again to drive the last pocket screw. Repeat this procedure for attaching the opposite skirt to the bench end.

Secure the right-angle jig to the bench end with a face clamp, being careful not to cover up the first pocket hole. Then face-clamp the jig to the benchtop.

Drive the first screw into the end, remove the right-angle jig, and finish screwing off the end to the top.

Now you can attach the other end. Measure and mark the benchtop to center the bench end in the same manner as before. Place the end against the skirts and clamp the 2½-in. spacer tight behind it to keep the end from being pushed out when driving the pocket screws.

Carefully drive the lower pocket screw from the skirt into the end on both sides (see the top left photo on p. 27). Drive the upper pocket screws from the skirt into the end, and finish by driving the pocket screws from the end into the benchtop.

Clamp a 1-in. spacer to the benchtop, then butt the skirt to the spacer and clamp in place.

Drive the screws through the skirt into the bench end, starting with the bottom screw, which is backed up by the 1-in. spacer.

Drive the screws from the skirt into the end on both sides.

Finish attaching the end by driving pocket screws into the top.

To install the shelf, make a pair of spacer jigs to support it.

Mark the location of the shelf at the front edge so that you can verify that the shelf did not shift when clamping the right-angle jig in place.

INSTALLING THE LOWER SHELF

I used 2¾-in. offcuts from the shelf strips plus pieces of 9-in. by 9¾-in. plywood to make a spacer jig to install the lower shelf. The jig needs to be in two parts so that the shelf does not get scratched when you remove the spacers. Place the plywood pieces with the 9¾-in. length going up and down against the bench ends. Set the 2¾-in. strips on top of the plywood pieces. Center the shelf on the ends by lining up the middle seam on the shelf with the middle seam on the ends. Since this seam will be hidden by the right-angle jig, make a mark on the underside of the shelf and the bench end to record the location of the shelf at the front edge.

Clamp the right-angle jig to the shelf and bench end so that the first pocket hole is uncovered.

Remove the right-angle jig and drive the rest of the screws through the shelf.

Hold the upper spacer in place as you slide out the lower spacer to keep from scratching the top of the shelf.

Attach the right-angle jig to the end and the shelf with face clamps so that the first pocket hole is visible. Make sure that the shelf didn't shift by checking the marks at the front. Drive the first pocket screw, then remove the jig and drive the remaining screws. Repeat this procedure at the other end. To keep from scratching the shelf, hold the top spacer in place with your hand or a clamp and then remove the lower spacer. At this point, the bench is assembled and ready for finish. To finish my bench, I applied four coats of Daly's® ProFin™ satin oil with a rag.

MIRROR AND PICTURE FRAME

Pocket hole joinery provides a quick and easy way to join boards on edge, and the mirror and picture frame projects presented here take full advantage of the pocket screw face-frame joint. You don't get the weakness of screwing into end grain, which can cause splitting, and there is no limit to the width of the boards you can join. Best of all, the holes are hidden on the backside of the work, which means that there's no need to plug countersunk screws.

Housed butt joints and stepped-thickness joints are details that work well with pocket screws. Combining pocket holes with dado-housed butt joints adds a fun aesthetic detail that highlights the intersection of the top rail with the stiles. The bottom rail on both projects steps down in thickness from ¾ in. to ⅝ in., which eliminates the need for flush-sanding and gluing. A square peg detail adds a bit of contrast and further interest to these two projects.

Stock Preparation

The mirror and picture frame involve similar construction techniques, varying only in the fact that the mirror has a shelf. For both projects,

MIRROR MATERIALS

QUANTITY	PART	ACTUAL SIZE	CONSTRUCTION NOTES
1	Top rail	¾ in. × 2½ in. × 31½ in.	Black walnut
2	Stiles	¾ in. × 2 in. × 19¼ in.	Black walnut
1	Bottom rail	⅝ in. × 2½ in. × 26½ in.	Black walnut
1	Shelf	¾ in. × 3¾ in. × 28 in.	Black walnut
2	Corbels	¾ in. × 1¼ in. × 3¾ in.	Black walnut
8	Pegs	⅜ in. × ⅜ in. × 5⁄16 in.	Pear

PICTURE FRAME MATERIALS

QUANTITY	PART	ACTUAL SIZE	CONSTRUCTION NOTES
1	Top rail	¾ in. × 1¾ in. × 13¾ in.	Red oak
2	Stiles	¾ in. × 1¾ in. × 9¾ in.	Red oak
1	Bottom rail	⅝ in. × 1¾ in. × 9¼ in.	Red oak
1	Shelf	¾ in. × 3¾ in. × 28 in.	Red oak
2	Corbels	¾ in. × 1¾ in. × 3¾ in.	Red oak
8	Pegs	⅜ in. × ⅜ in. × 5⁄16 in.	Red oak

start by milling all the stock to ¾ in. thick. Separate out the wood that will be used for the bottom rail, and continue to plane it until it is ⅝ in. thick to create the stepped thickness joint between the bottom rail and the stiles. Cut the top rail and stiles to length, leaving the bottom rail and shelf long for now. The mirror has two ¼-in. by 2-in. dadoes in the top rail, and each stile has a ¾-in. by ¾-in. dado to house the shelf. The picture frame has two ¼-in. by 1¾-in. dadoes in the top rail. Both the mirror and picture frame have a ½-in. overhang of the top rail over the stiles. This ½-in. inset detail is repeated where the bottom rail meets the stiles.

CUTTING THE DADOES

Start by marking the location of the dado on the top rail. Set a saw stop against the fence so that the first pass over the dado blade leaves ½ in. of wood remaining at the end of the top rail. Also, to minimize blowout, use a scrap of wood to back up the cut (see the top left photo on p. 32). Make the first pass on each end. Measure over the width of the stiles and make a mark locating the inside edge of the dado. Continue to make passes over the dado blade as you approach the end mark. I like to sneak up on the mark by making very light passes and checking the fit. A tight fit is okay, but if it's

MIRROR/PICTURE FRAME

Mirror

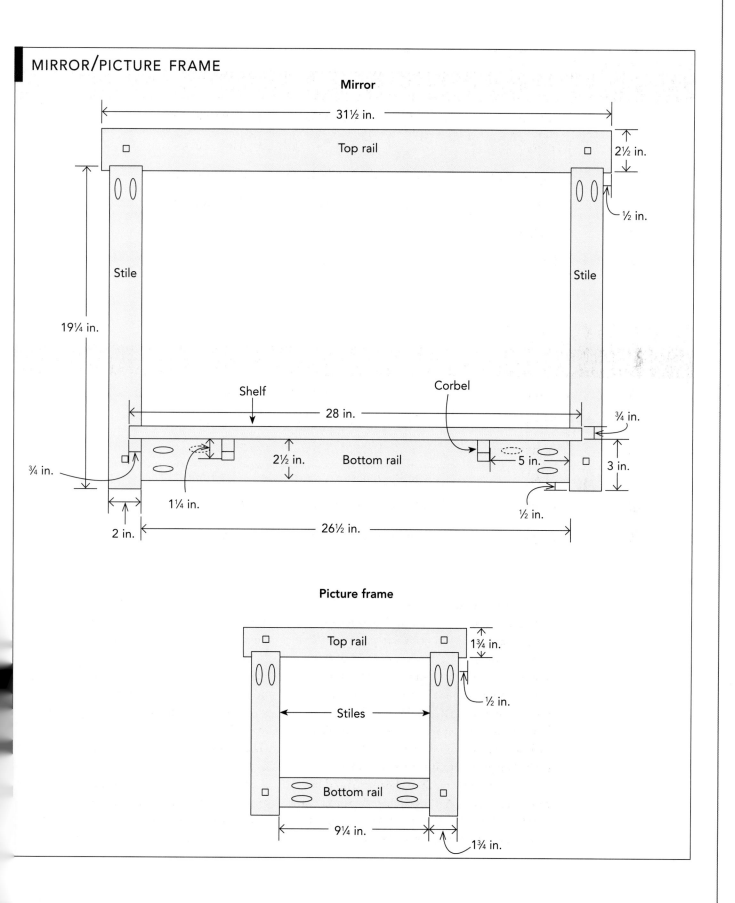

31½ in.

Top rail

2½ in.

½ in.

Stile

Stile

19¼ in.

Shelf

Corbel

28 in.

¾ in.

2½ in.

Bottom rail

5 in.

3 in.

¾ in.

1¼ in.

½ in.

2 in.

26½ in.

Picture frame

Top rail

1¾ in.

½ in.

Stiles

Bottom rail

9¼ in.

1¾ in.

To prepare to cut the first dado in the top rail, set a saw stop against the fence and use a scrap of ¼-in. plywood against the miter gauge to help back up the cut and minimize blowout.

After making the first pass on each end, measure over the width of the stiles and mark the inside edge of the dado.

Continue to make passes over the dado blade, stopping just shy of the pencil mark.

Check the fit between the stile and the top rail.

Measure up 3 in. from the end of the stile to mark the location of the shelf dado on the mirror.

too tight, you risk breaking off the small ½ in. of wood on the outside edge of the dado.

The mirror stiles have a dado to house the end of the shelf. The bottom edge of the dado is 3 in. up from the bottom of the stile (see the photo at left). Set the dado blade at ¾ in. high and set a stop block 3 in. from the blade. Make a cut in a scrap piece of wood to check your measurements. If the blade and fence settings are correct, make a pass over the dado blade. Use the shelf thickness measurement to mark the width of the dado and make small passes as you approach this mark, checking the fit once you get close.

Cut the shelf dado in the mirror stile (left), checking the fit once you get close (right).

Set the stiles into the dadoes in the top rail, and measure the inside width between the stiles to calculate the exact length of the bottom rail.

CUTTING THE BOTTOM RAIL AND SHELF

To calculate the length of the bottom rail, measure the distance between the inside edge of the dadoes on the top rail. Cut the bottom rail to length, then dry-fit the assembly to determine the length of the shelf. Set the saw stop and cut a scrap piece of wood to check the fit. Cut the shelf to length and dry-fit the pieces again.

CUTTING THE CORBEL DADOES

The bottom rail on the mirror has two small corbels that help support the shelf. They are housed in 1¼-in.-deep by ¾-in. dadoes in the

Dry-fit the frame to measure the length of the shelf. A clamp across the stiles will help hold the assembly together to ensure an accurate measurement.

Use the corbel material to gauge the width of the corbel dadoes in the bottom rail.

Cutting Square Peg Holes

There are a couple of ways to make square peg holes. The easiest is to use a hollow-chisel mortising machine, an expensive tool that's not found in a lot of woodshops. The second is to drill a hole with a ⅜-in. brad-point bit and use the outer square chisel from a mortising bit with a mallet to square off the hole (as shown on p. 35). The third option is to drill a hole with a ⅜-in. brad-point bit and use a ⅜-in. chisel to square off the hole.

The advantage of the mortise bit either in a machine or with a mallet is that all the square holes will be the same size. With a chisel, each hole will be slightly different and thus require more work to size the square pegs. Another option is to simply use round protruding plugs to fill the holes, which would still be very attractive.

bottom rail. Set the dado blade at 1¼ in. high and the stop block so that the dado starts 5 in. from the edge of the bottom rail. Make a pass on each end and then, using the corbel material thickness, mark the inside edge of the dado cut. Use the same process of making small passes and checking the fit to finish off the cut.

Laying Out the Peg Holes

The mirror and the picture frame both have square peg details at the corners. On the picture frame, the pegs are purely cosmetic and can be omitted. On the mirror, the pegs hide the screws used for installation and for holding the shelf to the corbels. The pegs on the top rail are centered above the dado; on the stiles, they are centered directly across from the bottom rail; and on the shelf, the pegs are centered above the corbels.

CUTTING THE PEG HOLES

As explained in the sidebar at left, there are a number of ways to cut square peg holes. I use a ⅜-in. brad-point bit with the outer square

Mark the center of the peg holes on the picture frame.

Drill out the center of the hole with a ⅜-in. brad-point bit.

Use a try square to mark the outer edges of the peg holes to help align the square chisel mortiser.

Set the chisel on the marks and pound gently with a mallet.

Once the peg hole has been started, finish off wood removal with a ⅜-in. chisel.

chisel from a mortising bit. Drill the holes ¼ in. deep. Then use a square to mark the outside edge of the hole to help align the square chisel. Pound the square chisel until it makes a complete mark around the hole and then clean up with a standard ⅜-in. chisel.

Milling the Rabbets

With the peg holes cut, it's time to mill the rabbet that houses the mirror or picture frame. For the picture frame, I purchased a cheap frame for the glass and backing and discarded the frame

RABBET AND CORBEL DETAILS

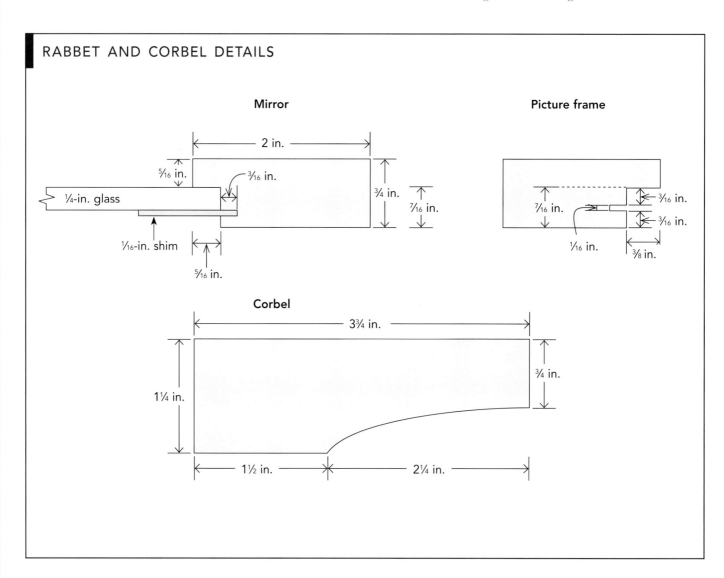

Mirror

2 in.

5⁄16 in.

3⁄16 in.

¼-in. glass

¾ in.

7⁄16 in.

1⁄16-in. shim

5⁄16 in.

Picture frame

3⁄16 in.

7⁄16 in.

3⁄16 in.

1⁄16 in.

⅜ in.

Corbel

3¾ in.

1¼ in.

¾ in.

1½ in.

2¼ in.

Use a chisel to square off the end of the stopped rabbets.

A ⅟₁₆-in. shim holds the mirror in place.

The author used the backing (and glass) from an inexpensive store-bought picture frame.

itself. The depth of the rabbet depends on the material used to hold the picture in place. The mirror uses ¼-in. glass, with short pieces of ⅟₁₆-in. by 1-in. by 2-in. shims placed around the perimeter to hold it in place. I cut the shim hole with a ⅟₁₆-in. slot cutter; a circular saw blade mounted in the tablesaw will give similar results. The rabbet for the mirror measures ⁵⁄₁₆ in. wide by ⁷⁄₁₆ in. deep, and for the picture frame, ⅜ in. wide by ⁷⁄₁₆ in. deep. I milled the stop-cut rabbet on the router table, using the

dadoes in the top rail and stiles to help start and stop the cuts.

The shelf on the mirror also gets a rabbet cut, but the stock is oriented with the face of the shelf against the router table fence. Make a mark on the router fence showing where the bit starts and stops the cut, then make corresponding marks on the frame parts for the start and end of the rabbet. There may be some chiseling needed on the top rail where the stiles enter the notch and on the stiles of the picture frame.

Drill two pocket holes into the backside of the bottom rail of the mirror and two holes on the tops of the stiles.

If you can fit the jig onto the bottom rail, you can use pocket screws to secure the corbels.

Next, rout the slots for the shims on the mirror and for hooking the backing on the picture frame. On the mirror, the shims are ¼ in. off the bottom of the rabbet. Use a scrap piece of ¼-in. glass or wood to align the cut (see the top right photo on p. 37). Two slots on the sides and three across the bottom and top of the mirror will be plenty to ensure a tight fit. On my pic-ture frame, the backing slid into one stile and small swivel tabs slid into the opposite stile. No slots were needed on the top and bottom rail.

Drilling the Pocket Holes

Now it's time to drill holes for the pocket screws on the stiles and bottom rail. You will need to space the pocket holes close together so they don't protrude into the rabbet or shim slots. Drill two holes on the top of the stiles and two holes on either end of the bottom rail for both the mirror and picture frame.

The bottom rail of the mirror has two notches for the corbels to fit into. It is possible to pocket-screw the corbels into place (the other option would be simply to screw down through the corbel into the bottom rail). You'll need to use the portable pocket screw jig and align the face clamp on the side of the jig, not in the usual circular slot. This is just another fun application of pocket screws that doesn't fall into the normal category but shows how versatile the jig can be.

Round over and chamfer the notches and square peg holes to make these details stand out and to aid in assembly.

Making the pegs of a contrasting wood (here, pear) adds a handmade detail to the project.

CHAMFERING THE DETAILS

I like to accentuate all the notches with a file. This makes the notch detail stand out and helps with assembling the prefinished pieces. I also like to chamfer the square peg holes for added effect. Round over and chamfer these areas after the machine marks have been cleaned up but before the final finish sanding. I sand with 120 grit followed by 180 grit and then round over the edges with a block plane and chamfer the pegs and notches, finishing with a final sanding of 220 grit.

FITTING THE PEGS

Making the pegs of a contrasting wood ensures that they'll be noticed; for the mirror, I used pear for the plugs and black walnut for the frame. If you used a mortising chisel, chances are that all the square holes are the same size, so making pegs is just a matter of milling some ⅜-in. by ⅜-in. strips and rounding and finish-sanding the ends (leave the peg stock long until

final assembly). If you hand-chiseled the square holes, you may need to make a few strips that vary slightly from the ⅜-in. by ⅜-in. dimensions. Since all of the shoulders of the square peg holes have been chamfered, a loose-fitting peg will not be noticed.

Prefinishing is not mandatory but more a personal preference. This would be a great time to apply the finish of your choice (I used four coats of Daley's ProFin satin oil), but waiting till after the mirror is assembled is also an option.

Assembling the Mirror

To assemble the mirror, start with the corbels in the bottom rail. Clamp them into place with the end grain of the corbel slightly shy of the back surface and slowly drive the pocket screw. Repeat on the other side.

Clamp the top rail to the right-angle jig. Use the face clamp to clamp a stile into place, making sure that the shelf dado is facing in. Drive two pocket screws into the top rail and repeat

Clamp the corbel to the bottom rail, holding the end of the corbel slightly shy of the back face of the rail to ensure it won't stick out past the face once screwed.

Clamping the corbels slightly shy of the back of the bottom rail compensates for the slight shift that sometimes occurs when pocket screwing. By anticipating the shift, you'll guarantee that the end grain of the corbel doesn't stick out past the bottom rail.

Attach the face clamp over the housed joint, and drive pocket screws into the top rail.

the procedure for the opposite stile. Carefully place the partially assembled mirror face up on the bench and slide the shelf into place. Position the bottom rail under the shelf and orient the assembly so that one of the lower corners overhangs the bench. Since the stiles and bottom rail differ in thickness, a ⅛-in. shim will be needed during clamping. To ensure that the backs are flush, place the ⅛-in. shim on top of the bottom rail, which makes it the same thickness as the stiles. Clamp the stile/rail butt joint with the face clamp. Slowly drive two pocket screws into the stile. After one side of the bottom rail is screwed, repeat the process for the opposite side.

Hang the bottom corner of the frame over the edge of the bench to provide access for clamping and driving the pocket screws.

Predrill the shelf and corbel before driving the screw.

Remove the dry-fit shelf from the frame and stand the mirror up, holding the mirror upright by clamping either stile to the right-angle jig. Slide the shelf back into position, making sure that the rabbet on the backside matches up with the rabbet on the stiles. Carefully predrill one shelf peg hole into a corbel and drive a #10 by ¾-in. screw. If the shelf shifted during screwing, back out the screw and try again with the other peg hole. Repeat for the other side. With the shelf now held in place, predrill and screw the two remaining peg holes. You can also fit a couple of screws through the rabbet of the shelf into the lower rail, which helps pull out any gaps between the two. Make sure to completely countersink the screw heads in the rabbet so that the mirror will not touch any metal when installed.

With the mirror frame assembled, you can confidently order the ¼-in. glass. Measure the rough opening and subtract ⅛ in. from the height and width. By taking the mirror frame to the glass shop when ordering, you will also ensure a correct fit.

An additional screw through the rabbet of the shelf into the bottom rail helps close up any gaps between the two and adds some strength.

Use a strip of wood to back up the cut on the peg stock to help keep the cut square and to keep your fingers a safe distance from the blade.

Tap the pegs into place with a leather-covered mallet head.

INSTALLING THE PEGS

It's easiest to leave the peg stock long while finishing and sanding between coats and then cut the pegs to length right before assembly. Cutting a 5/16-in.-long peg can be tricky. It's safest to use a handsaw, but it can be hard to get a perfectly square cut. An option is to make the cut on a bandsaw, with the peg strip backed up with a longer strip of wood to keep your fingers a safe distance from the blade. Once the pegs are cut, chamfer the bottom edges lightly with a file to help them seat into the square peg hole. Gently tap into place with a leather-covered mallet head.

The pegs in the shelf can be installed at this point, but leave the corner pegs out for now. You can use the four corner holes and drywall anchors to hang the mirror and then plug the holes after it's hung. This provides a strong four-point attachment to the wall, but it does make it difficult to change the mirror's location. If you need to move the mirror, carefully pry the plugs up with a chisel and leather protecting pad. Pry one side then another side, alternating back and forth. A looser-fitting corner plug is better than a tight-fitting one for this reason. If a plug is really tight, you'll need to drill a small 1/16-in. hole in the center of the plug. Then thread a screw into the hole and use a pair of pliers to grab the screw head to help pull out the plug. This destroys the plug, of course, which is a good reason to make an extra set of plugs.

INSTALLING THE HANGERS

For additional utility, I installed coat hangers along the bottom rail of the mirror. Four hooks pretty much fill up the space. I center the first and last hook between the outside edge of the corbel and the end of the bottom rail. The second and third hooks are then centered between the first and last hook or about 7 1/8 in. on-center.

If you need to remove the corner plugs from the mirror, carefully pry them up with a chisel, using a leather pad to protect the frame.

Press the shims into the kerfs in the frame to hold the mirror in place.

Hanging the Mirror

To install the mirror, flip the frame face down on a protective blanket. Cut a handful of $\frac{1}{16}$-in. by 1-in. by 2-in.-long strips. Lay the mirror into the dado, and press the $\frac{1}{16}$-in. shims into the kerfs, as shown in the photo at right.

You're almost ready to hang the mirror, but first drill out the corner peg holes with a $\frac{3}{16}$-in. or smaller drill bit. Position the mirror in its location, and drive one top corner screw into the wall. Drive it just deep enough to hold the mirror in place. Level the mirror and drive a screw into the opposite top corner. Mark the bottom two holes with the drill bit, but don't drive a screw yet. If there isn't any framing material to hold the screws in the wall, you'll need to install drywall anchors. Remove the screws and the mirror from the wall, and drive the anchors into the holes. Replace the mirror onto the wall, and drive the screws in tight. Finish the installation by plugging the square peg corner holes.

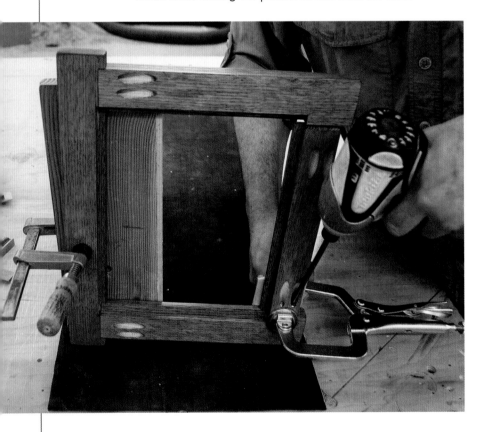

Use the right-angle jig to hold the top rail of the picture frame while driving the pocket screws from the stile.

Assembling the Picture Frame

The picture frame follows the same construction procedure as the mirror. Clamp the top rail to the right-angle jig and clamp a stile with the face clamp into the dado housing. Slowly drive a screw into each hole. Take a look at the square peg hole to see if the screw tip is poking out. With so many things packed into such a small area, chances are good you'll see the screw tip. If this happens, back it out and use a shorter 1-in. screw. Alternatively, simply grind off the tip (which is what I did). Repeat this procedure for the opposite stile.

For the bottom rail, orient the frame onto its side and clamp the top rail to the right-angle jig. Align the bottom rail ½ in. up from the bottom edge of the stile, and clamp with the face clamp and ⅛-in. shim in front. Slowly drive a screw. Be extra careful when two pocket screws are so tightly packed together: It is entirely possible that the wood could split, especially if there is a knot. In situations like this, it's safest to predrill for the second screw. Repeat for the other end of the bottom rail.

The picture frame will be hung using the frame backing, so go ahead and plug the four corner holes with the pegs. Cut the pegs ⁵⁄₁₆ in. long on the bandsaw. Chamfer the bottom edge of the peg on a file to help it seat in the square peg hole. Gently tap the pegs into place with a leather-tipped mallet or similar protective surface. Flip the frame over and insert the glass and picture. Slide the picture backing into the ¹⁄₁₆-in. kerf on one side of the frame, then twist the locking tabs on the opposite side into place.

Carefully drive the tightly spaced screws into the bottom rail. Predrilling with a ⅛-in. extra-long bit goes a long way in reducing the stress.

After cutting the peg to length, file a slight chamfer on the underside to help it seat in the mortise.

Small swivel tabs on the picture frame backing engage into the $1/16$-in. kerf to hold the backing in place.

4 BUILT-IN BOOKCASE

Built-ins are a perfect project for pocket screws. With one face visible and one hidden from view, finding a spot for pocket holes is simple. Normally, it's about trying to hide screws on the inside, but with built-ins all the pocket holes are on the outside, so they are easy to reach. The bookcase box is made from ¾-in. maple plywood. The

MATERIALS

QUANTITY	PART	ACTUAL SIZE	CONSTRUCTION NOTES
FRONT FACE FRAME			
1	Top rail	¾ in. × 3½ in. × 44⅜ in.	Maple
2	Stiles	¾ in. × 3½ in. × 35⁹⁄₁₆ in.	Maple
1	Bottom rail	¾ in. × 3½ in. × 36 in.	Maple
BACK FRAME			
2	Stiles	¾ in. × 3 in. × 33½ in.	Maple
2	Rails	¾ in. × 3 in. × 31½ in.	Maple
1	Plywood panel	¼ in. × 28 in. × 32 in.	Maple plywood
PLYWOOD BOX			
2	Sides	¾ in. × 11¾ in. × 31½ in.	Maple plywood
2	Top and bottom	¾ in. × 11¾ in. × 37½ in.	Maple plywood
2	Shelves	¾ in. × 12 in. × 36 in.	Maple

face frame, back frame, and shelves are ¾-in. solid maple, and the back panel is ¼-in. maple plywood. Mill up the maple to thickness and width, but leave the lengths long until after the box is assembled.

Building the Box

Start with the construction of the plywood box. The top and bottom panels get pocket holes on the front and back edges only, whereas the side panels get pocket holes along all four edges (see the drawing on p. 48). The corners are usually the only areas where careful layout of pocket holes is important to ensure that the screws do not land on top of each other. Along the edge that attaches the face frame, start with a pocket hole at 2 in., then every 8 in. to 10 in. on-center. For the sides that attach to the top and bottom panels, four holes should be plenty, starting at

A built-in is a perfect project for pocket hole joinery, as all the pocket holes are on the concealed outside of the piece. From the back, it's easy to see how the case was assembled.

BUILT-IN BOOKCASE

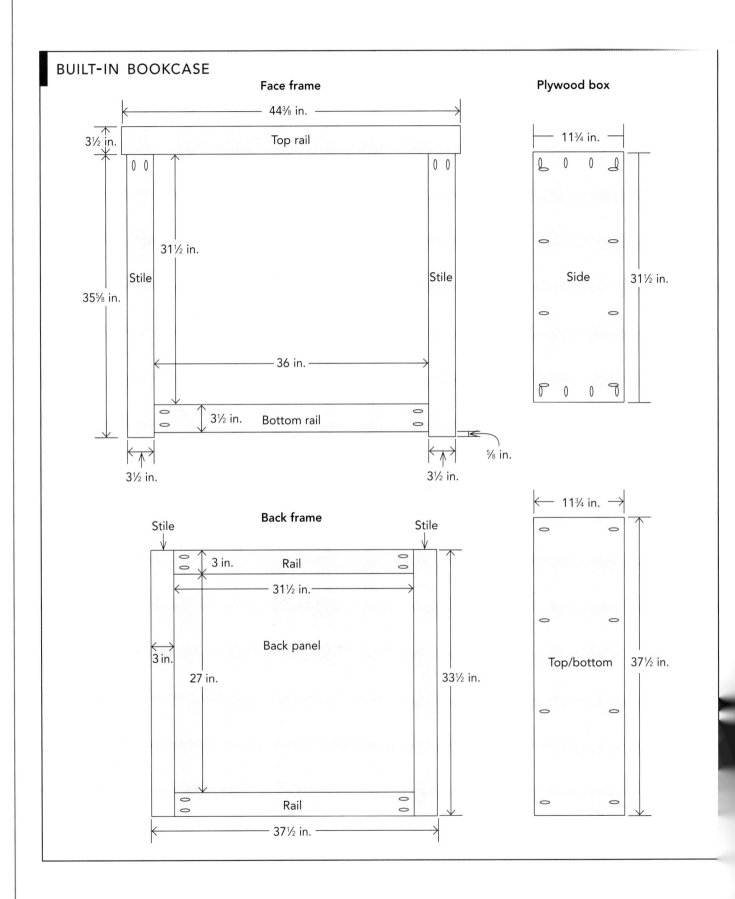

Face frame

44⅜ in.

Top rail

3½ in.

Stile

31½ in.

35⅝ in.

Stile

36 in.

3½ in.   Bottom rail

⅝ in.

3½ in.

3½ in.

Plywood box

11¾ in.

Side

31½ in.

11¾ in.

Top/bottom

37½ in.

Back frame

Stile

Stile

3 in.   Rail

31½ in.

Back panel

3 in.

27 in.

33½ in.

Rail

37½ in.

The author uses the Kreg Foreman machine to drill out the built-in plywood parts, but any pocket screw jig will work.

1 in. and 4 in. from the front and back edge. Drill out all the pocket holes on the plywood parts at this time.

To support the shelves, you'll need to drill shelf pin holes in the box sides. Depending on the jig that you use, it may be necessary to drill for the shelf pins before assembly. The jig I used has two sets of five holes centered at 11 in. and 22 in. Set the jig to drill the holes about 2 in. from the front plywood edge, clearly avoiding the case pocket holes (see the top left photo on p. 50).

To begin assembly of the box, clamp the right-angle jig to a side and set it on top of the bottom plywood piece. Flush up the corner and clamp the right-angle jig to the plywood bottom and benchtop to hold it secure. The best way to secure the side is to use bar clamps across the joint positioned above the pocket holes, but there is a good alternative when either a bar clamp of the needed length is not available or it is too awkward to clamp onto the cabinet. Simply screw a small block of plywood to the vertical side at the edge of the pocket hole,

Shelf Pin Jigs

There are several different commercial shelf pin jigs available; they use either a drill bit or a router bit to drill the holes. Router bits always leave a very clean hole, whereas drill bits tend to tear out just a hair on at least one hole. However, router bit jigs are more time-consuming to set up and use. The key to drilling shelf pins is to clearly label the parts to be drilled and to make sure the jig is referenced to the right face when clamping it to the parts.

You can also build your own shelf pin jig out of ¼-in. plywood, though shop-built jigs usually only hold up for one cabinet before the holes get too reamed out to be accurate. For shop-built jigs, make sure to label the front and bottom edges and keep them oriented the same as you drill either side of the cabinet.

Use a shelf pin jig to drill the holes in the sides of the cabinet.

You can use the right-angle jig and small blocks of wood instead of a bar clamp to secure the side to the bottom while pocket screwing.

Use bar clamps to hold the top panel in place while screwing.

which will prohibit the side from shifting when driving the pocket screw. Finish assembling the box.

Building the Back Panel

To construct the back frame, you'll need an adjustable pocket jig with a ½-in. thickness setting and some 1½-in. fine-thread screws. (If you're using a standard nonadjustable jig, the groove for the plywood panel must be a stop cut. For information about frame-and-panel construction using a stop cut, refer to the end-panel construction technique in the Vanity project on p. 140.)

Measure the constructed outside width and height of the cabinet. The back-panel stiles are the same height as the box. The rails are the outside box width minus 6 in., the combined width of the stiles. Cut the back frame material to length (see "Materials" on p. 47). The ¼-in. plywood back panel will be centered on the ¾-in. frame material. The simplest way to cut the groove for the panel is to make multiple passes over the tablesaw. Label the fronts of the frame material. Set the tablesaw fence at ¼ in. and the blade height at 5/16 in. With the front faces of the frame stock against the saw fence, make a pass over the blade without stopping.

Adjust the pocket screw jig to the ½-in. material thickness setting to drill the back-panel rails for use with 1½-in. screws.

Change the stop collar setting to ½ in. for drilling the rails for use with 1½-in. screws.

Using longer screws and the ½-in. thickness setting ensures a stronger connection.

Drill the back-panel rails with the adjusted drill bit and jig.

Check the fit of the frame and panel before finish sanding and assembly.

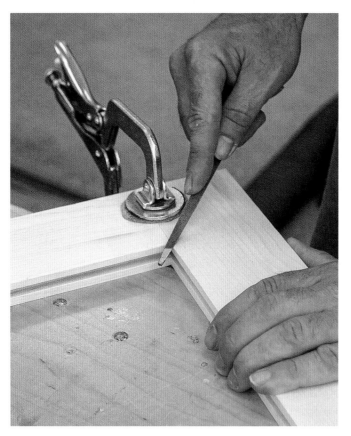

Chamfer the inside corner of the back frame panel with a triangle file before assembly (the spot is hard to reach once the frame and panel are assembled).

Begin the back-panel assembly with the rails and panel dry-fit, and apply glue to the joint between the stiles and the rails.

Bump the saw fence over 1/16 in. and make another pass; check the fit with a scrap of the 1/4-in. back-panel material. Continue to bump the fence over and check the fit until the back-panel scrap slides smoothly in the groove.

The rails get pocket holes on either end. To allow for the 1 1/2-in.-long screws on 3/4-in. stock

Make sure to have a clamp directly above both pocket holes when driving a pocket screw into the back frame joints.

thickness, you need to set the adjustable pocket jig and stop collar on the drill bit to the ½-in. stock thickness setting (see the top left photo on p. 51). By shifting the pocket hole location and using longer screws, you can line up the screw directly above the panel groove and with the added ¼-in. length of the screw get plenty of purchase. After drilling the pocket holes in the top and bottom rails, make sure to reset the jig and stop collar to ¾ in. so as not to improperly drill the remaining ¾-in. stock on the face frame.

To get the panel size, dry-fit the back frame and add ½ in. to the inside dimension of the frame. Cut the panel to size and check the fit (see the top right photo on the facing page). Round over the edges on the rails from end to end. Hold the joint between the rails and stiles with a face clamp to mark where the roundover on the stiles stops. Mark it with a file. Remove the face clamps and round over the stiles

between the file marks. Clean up the inside edge on the frame material, which will be hard to reach after the frame and panel is assembled.

Whenever two surfaces are supposed to remain flush after pocket screwing, it's important to glue the joint. This isn't so much an issue of strength as it is to keep the flush-sanded surface from shifting and creating a ridge. Center the top and bottom rails on the panel. Apply glue to the joint area of the stile. It's important to clamp directly above the pocket hole to be screwed, so for this reason it's nice to have a couple of face clamps. Slide the stile into place and clamp above a pocket hole on each end with the face clamps. Slowly drive the screw. Leave the clamps on for a few minutes so that the glue has time to tack up. Then carefully remove the clamps and repeat the process with the other stile. Let the joints dry completely before sanding flush.

Drill the bottom rail with pocket holes on both ends after drilling the top ends of the stiles.

Assembling the Front Face Frame

To achieve what looks like a flush edge at the front of the built-in, make the inside width and height of the face frame $\frac{1}{16}$ in. less than the inside dimensions of the cabinet. This will give a $\frac{1}{32}$-in. overhang on either side, which will for all purposes appear flush. To help assemble the front face frame to these tolerances, you need to use spacers. Measure the inside width of the cabinet at the top and bottom. Subtract $\frac{1}{16}$ in. from this measurement, set a saw stop block to this length, and cut a plywood strip. Check the plywood strip inside the cabinet along the bottom and top edge to make sure it's the right size. If the fit is good, cut the bottom rail to length using the stop block set for the spacer. It's important that the bottom rail and horizontal spacer are the same length. Next, measure the inside height of the cabinet, subtract $\frac{1}{16}$ in., set a saw stop to this measurement, and cut two plywood strips. Double-check their fit inside the cabinet on both sides.

The stiles extend past the bottom edge of the bottom rail by $\frac{5}{8}$ in. Take the length of the verti-

WORK SMART

To center the spacer, measure from the end of the spacer to the end of the top rail on both ends. The spacer is centered when these measurements are the same.

Clamp the top spacer to the top rail to locate the stiles exactly $\frac{1}{16}$ in. less than the cabinet opening, then attach the stile to the top rail with two pocket screws.

Using the vertical spacers as locating jigs, attach the bottom rail with pocket screws and face clamps.

With the front frame assembled, check the fit on top of the cabinet. It should just barely overhang the plywood core.

cal spacer, add the width of the bottom rail, and then add ⁵⁄₈ in. to determine the length of the stiles. On this cabinet, the stiles are 4¹⁄₈ in. longer than the plywood spacers; cut them to length now. The top rail is the length of the horizontal spacer, plus twice the stile width plus 1¼ in. (⁵⁄₈-in. overhang on both sides); cut to length now. With the pocket screw jig set for ¾-in. stock thickness, drill two pocket holes on the inside top edge of the stiles. Drill two pocket holes on both ends of the bottom rail. The top rail does not get drilled for pocket holes. Clean up any machine marks on the edges of the face frame material that will be hard to reach after assembly, but do not round over any corners yet.

To assemble, start by centering and clamping the horizontal spacer to the top rail with the back side up. Apply glue to the end of a stile, and locate it tight against the spacer. Use face clamps to hold the joint tight while driving pocket screws. Give the glue a few minutes to set up before removing the face clamps. Repeat with the other stile. To locate the bottom rail, clamp a vertical spacer to each stile butted tight against the top rail. Apply glue to both ends of the bottom rail, and slide it into place. Hold

Lightly sand the inside edge of the frame to soften the step between the frame and plywood sides.

tight with face clamps while driving the screws. Repeat on the opposite end. Let the glue dry completely before sanding the butt joints flush.

Place the front frame on top of the cabinet to check that the frame completely covers the plywood core. I gently ease over the inside edge on the frame with sandpaper. On the cabinet, just touch the plywood edge with sandpaper to take off the sharp edge.

Clamp the lower corner of the frame to the box, using cauls to protect the surface. Center the frame so there's an equal overhang on all four sides.

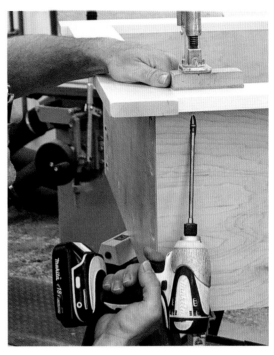

Drive the first screw in the lower corner, and check to see how much (if any) shift occurred.

Straightening the Sides

Sometimes you need another pocket hole to help pull the plywood sides into alignment. This small pocket jig can be screwed directly to the cabinet sides to drill a pocket hole without disassembly.

Sometimes the plywood cores have a slight bow where there are no pocket holes and you're unable to get the attachment just right. Taking apart the face frame and drilling an additional hole in the location is an option but not one you really want to take. The small portable pocket hole jig shown here is great for just such a dilemma. It can be attached to an already assembled cabinet to add an additional pocket hole. It is especially effective in this situation, where the frame will appear to be flush with the cabinet and you need to pull the core out of view just a bit.

After the top and bottom fields have been screwed, move the cabinet to a bench. Clamp the sides and attach with pocket screws.

Installing the Front Frame

Set the front face frame on the box, centering it so that the slight overhang on the top/bottom and side to side is equal. Anticipate a slight shift for the first screw and nudge the face frame to compensate for the potential shift. (To gauge how much to shift it, I made the top of the frame almost flush with the top of the cabinet so that the bottom rail was clearly overhanging the bottom of the frame.) Clamp the lower corners, using protective pads (or wood cauls) to prevent marring from the clamps. Drive the first screw from below. Did it shift? If not, and you anticipated shift, gently tap the plywood with a mallet to the desired location. You can always tap in the direction of the screw angle but you cannot tap back. So by anticipating shift, you can always come out ahead even if there was no shift by tapping it into place. Repeat the procedure on the other lower corner. The next set of screws to be driven are the first holes on the vertical sides. Clamp and drive those screws, then follow the same procedure on the top corners.

When the corners are correctly attached, move on to the spans along the top and bottom edges. You can flex the plywood in the field to exactly line up the edge with the frame. Anticipate shift by clamping the plywood edge safely out of the way and then tapping it into location after the screw has been driven. After the top and bottom are secure, you can move the cabinet to a benchtop to drive the pocket screws into the stiles.

Use small scraps of paper towels to protect the back panel surface from scratches as the cabinet is set on top and centered.

Attaching the Back Panel

Clamping the back panel to the cabinet will be difficult if you don't have deep-throat clamps. Clamping is the most secure option, but using small blocks of wood as was done with assembling the box will work, too. The back needs to be very close in size to the cabinet; otherwise, it will pull it out of plumb when screwing with the blocks. If it ended up being larger than the cabinet back, trim its dimensions. If it is smaller than the cabinet, you can attach two sides using the blocks, which will hold the cabinet square while you clamp or use blocks and shims to make up the difference.

Lay the back panel face up on the benchtop. Set some paper towel scraps on the frame to protect the surface when centering the cabinet.

When the cabinet is located on the back panel, remove the paper towel scraps and attach a couple of cleats to the bench to keep it from sliding. Attach a block to the side next to the first hole at the corner. Attach another block on the opposite side of the corner. Drive the two pocket screws using downward hand pressure on the cabinet. Screw the corners first, then screw the field.

Cutting the Shelves

Measure the opening and cut the shelves to length, making them at least $1/16$ in. to $1/32$ in. shorter so that you don't scratch the sides when you install the shelves. Rarely do dimensions end up perfect, and custom-fitting the shelves is

Small blocks can help hold the cabinet in place if deep-throat clamps aren't available. A small shim under the block keeps the block up off the bench so that the seam between the cabinet and back panel can be pushed tight.

Drive a screw into the back panel; notice the gap under the block.

The case assembled . . . and not a single pocket screw visible.

The author used solid maple shelves for looks and strength.

a common task. Small amounts of wood may need to be removed from the shelf ends to make them square to the sides.

Installing the Cabinet

All that's left is to finish the cabinet (I used three coats of Daly's ProFin oil finish) and install it in the wall.

Installing the cabinet into the wall opening requires a solid platform for the cabinet to sit on and nailers along the sides. The easiest way to hide the fasteners is to use countersunk screws along the back of the bottom edge. Another option is to sneak screws into the shelf pin holes; the head of the screw needs to be very small though (you may need to grind the screwhead to fit).

Start by leveling the bottom of the cabinet. This requires installing the cabinet into the opening, checking for level, and then removing

the cabinet. Place a shim to correct the level and recheck. If there is a lot of room on either side of the cabinet, you'll need to install shims along the sides so that any screws from the cabinet into the framing do not pull it out of square.

Prefinishing a cabinet before installing the face frame [and cabinet] has its advantages, as applying finish in the tight corners can be cumbersome. But in this case, where only the inside needs finishing, it's not that big a chore to wait until the cabinet is built.

END TABLE

5

S mall projects like this end table can be very rewarding, and pocket screws can greatly simplify the building process. The challenges come in hiding the pocket screw holes and locating the parts during assembly. Using shims, clamps, and careful screw layout guarantees that the project will go together smoothly.

An end table is a perfect candidate for a simple design. A top, four legs, and a bottom shelf held together at the corners with a skirt—what could be easier? I usually start a project like this with a rough sketch. The size parameters and wood choice come next. For this end table, I try to keep it basic by making it square, but this also makes it plain, which detracts a bit from its overall appeal. A design that's sturdy rather than delicate seems appropriate for something this small, so I keep the leg dimensions as big as my 8/4 solid cherry stock will allow at 1¾ in. square. With a general idea of size—24 in. tall and 18 in. wide—I mill up the stock, leaving the skirt and stretchers long so that I can tweak the dimensions if need be. I stand up the legs in a square and place a scrap piece of plywood on top: ho-hum—it looks like a little box tower, not like the sketch I drew. I add another scrap of

QUANTITY	PART	ACTUAL SIZE	CONSTRUCTION NOTES
4	Legs	1¾ in. × 1¾ in. × 23 in.	Cherry
4	Skirts	¾ in. × 2½ in. × 12¾ in.	Cherry
2	Spacer side rails	¾ in. × 2 in. × 12¾ in.	Cherry
2	Spacer front and back	¾ in. × 1⅛ in. × 15 in.	Cherry
2	Lower stretchers	1⅜ in. × 1⅞ in. × 12¾ in.	Cherry
2	Shelf supports	¾ in. × 2 in. × 12¾ in.	Any wood (these are hidden from view)
1	Top	¾ in. × 18 in. × 18 in.	Cherry
1	Shelf	¾ in. × 12¾ in. × 15½ in.	Cherry

Using tape to mock up a design can help you flesh out ideas. Here, whether to cut a curve in the tabletop or leave it straight is decided using tape to represent the proposed shape.

wood propped up on blocks as the bottom shelf, which helps to ground it some.

I decide on an 18-in.-square top with a ⅞-in. overhang, which then gives me a skirt length of 12¾ in. by 2½ in. I cut the skirts to length and hold them in place with blue tape so that I can get an idea of what the finished table will look like. It still looks boxy. Straight lines on all four sides don't exactly make the table dance. I can either taper the legs at the bottom, which seems an unnecessary distraction, or maybe add a curve to the top on all four sides to add interest and soften its appearance. With more blue tape, I mock up a curve and stand back to fuss some more. While thinking about how I will attach the top to the skirt using pocket screws and dealing with wood movement, I come upon the idea of using a spacer between the table and top. Building a square frame, ⅝ in. smaller on all four sides, would lift the top and give it an interesting shadow line below. A couple of scraps placed on top of the legs give me just enough of an idea to visualize the effect. It's pleasing and I'm given the confidence to start laying out the pocket joinery.

Laying Out the Joinery

Whether using traditional joinery, dowels, or pocket screws, layout is always a critical first step. With pocket screws, you don't want a screw collision at the corners to weaken the joint or cause the leg or stretchers to split. On a large cabinet this isn't as much of a concern since there is usually room to shift a screw up or down, but on a small end table with the skirt coming in from either side, space is limited. Using cutoffs from the stock, I start by laying out all the screw locations at the corners and where the lower stretcher meets the legs. At the corners all I need is to avoid having the screws collide and keep them away from the ends so as not to promote splitting. On the lower stretcher, however, I have to make sure the pocket screw holes are hidden by the lower shelf but don't interfere with the shelf supports. Laying out the screw holes on paper and on a small mock-up will help keep the joinery from colliding. Mark the pocket screw hole locations at least 4½ in. from the end of the piece so that they can be seen over the top of the pocket screw jig when the stock is being clamped to drill.

Label the parts with cabinetmaker's triangles. The skirts have two pocket screw holes on either end drilled ½ in. on-center (o.c.) from the top and bottom edge (see the drawing on p. 65). Each leg has one pocket screw hole on the inside surface facing front or back; these holes are for the screws that will be used to hold the spacer frame in place. The spacer will be screwed to the

The author uses offcuts to mock up the pocket screw locations at the corners and where the lower stretcher meets the legs.

Marking with a cabinetmaker's triangle is a good way to keep track of all the parts.

Drill two pocket screw holes on either end of the skirts, spaced ½ in. o.c. from the top and bottom edge.

tabletop with oversize holes and washers to allow for wood movement and will be attached to the four legs at the corners. Drill this pocket screw hole ½ in. o.c. from the inside edge of the leg. The spacer has side rails 2 in. by 12¾ in. by ¾ in. The pocket screw holes are close together toward the inside edge to avoid the screw from the leg that secures the spacer to the table (see the drawing on the facing page). From the inside edge, drill the first hole ⅜ in. o.c. and the second hole ¹⁵⁄₁₆ in. o.c. The lower table support stretchers each get two pocket screw holes ⅝ in. o.c. from both edges on both ends.

The lower stretcher is 1⅜ in. thick going into a 1¾-in.-square leg. With dimensions this thick, it is possible (but not necessary) to use a longer screw. By raising the adjustable pocket screw jig to the 1⅜-in. setting and using a 2-in. screw, you can center the joint in the leg. Using two 1¼-in. screws won't provide as much strength as the 2-in. screw, but in this situation it's plenty adequate. If you already have an adjustable jig and some 2-in. screws, I suggest using them, but if you have a nonadjustable pocket screw jig and only the 1¼-in. screws, you'll be fine sticking with that. The pocket screw drill only countersinks for the head and about ½ in. of the shank, so using longer screws means there will be more wood for the

If you're using an adjustable pocket screw jig, you can raise the jig to the 1⅜-in. thickness setting so you can use a longer (2-in.) screw to attach the lower stretcher.

Drive the 2-in. screw through the hole in the stretcher to mark it for reaming with the extra-long ⅛-in. bit (left). Ream the hole (right).

END TABLE

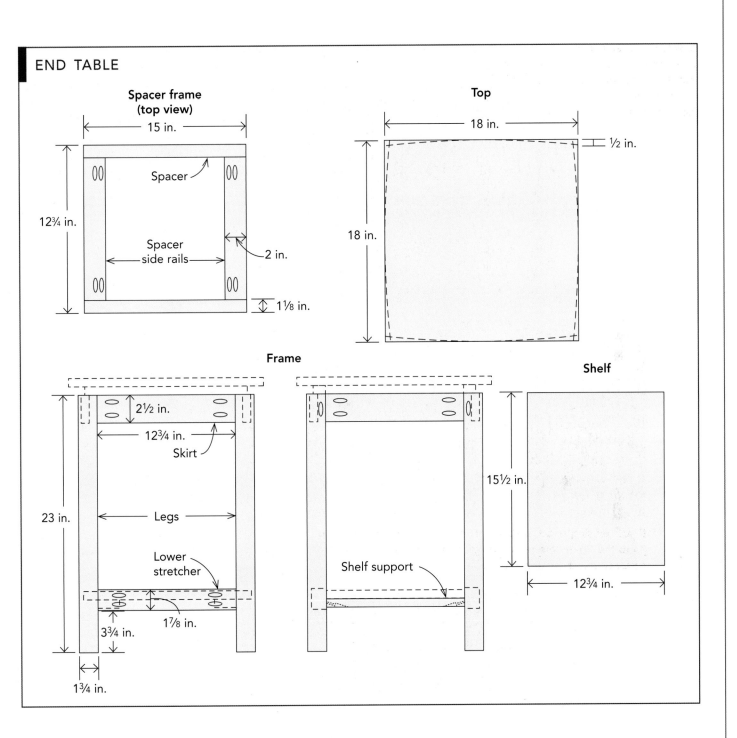

Spacer frame (top view)

15 in.

Spacer

12¾ in.

Spacer side rails

2 in.

1⅛ in.

Top

18 in.

½ in.

18 in.

Frame

2½ in.

12¾ in.

Skirt

23 in.

Legs

Lower stretcher

1⅞ in.

3¾ in.

1¾ in.

Shelf support

Shelf

15½ in.

12¾ in.

screw to drive through. Just to play it safe, I drive a 2-in. screw through the stretcher until the tip of the screw shows at the end, then back out the screw and ream out the hole with a drill bit. When driving the screws, I predrill ⅛ in. deep with an extra-long drill bit. This may be overkill, but it provides a buffer of security from the piece splitting or shifting during assembly. Locate the drill holes on the inside face of the stretcher ⅜ in. from the bottom edge and ⅝ in. from the top edge o.c.

Nothing gets rid of machine marks faster than a sharp handplane.

Mark the stretcher location on the legs to help you know where to stop and start the roundover edge on the leg.

Stock Cleanup

Just because you're building with pocket screws doesn't mean you can't use traditional techniques when appropriate. Handplane and scraper skills are invaluable. As you work through the stock cleanup, you will find it necessary to move the label marks as you sand. The top of the legs will be visible on the outside edge, so move the leg labels to the inside front side and include an arrow pointing up.

Sand the surfaces and round over all the edges except the inside edge of the legs. The inside face of the lower stretchers and the inside face of the legs are flush at the joint. With the leg face down on the bench, butt the lower stretcher against it 3¾ in. up from the bottom of the leg and make a mark on top and bottom of where the stretcher hits the leg. This will let you know when to stop and start the roundover of the inside edge. Place a small scrap of tape to remind you to stop. No roundover is required on the spacer between the legs and top. After the sides have been assembled, you can round over the edge exactly above and below the lower stretcher and flush-sand the butt joint.

In general, I prefer to prefinish the parts. On this project, however, the legs will need a flush sanding where the lower rail meets the leg. Also, there will be lots of clamping with spacers and bar clamps, which could mar the finish. So here the finish is best applied after the legs and skirts are assembled but before the top and shelf are installed.

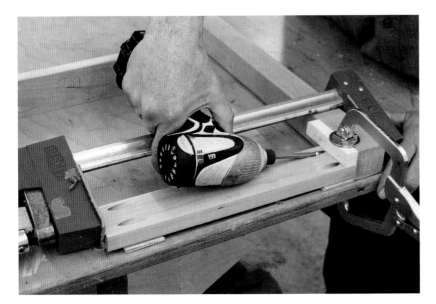

Use a bar clamp and a face clamp to hold the leg/skirt assembly in place while driving the pocket screws.

Use a square to locate the lower stretcher on the legs.

Assembling the Legs

To begin the assembly, start with a front leg and either the left or right 2½-in. skirt. There is a ³⁄₁₆-in. step between the face of the leg and the face of the skirt. (This is both a design detail and a pocket screw time-saver: By not having the surface of the skirt flush with the surface of the leg, there's no need for glue or flush-sanding.) Cut two small scraps of wood 2½ in. long and ³⁄₁₆ in. thick at least 1½ in. wide. You'll also need another shim for the back of the skirt so that the combined width of the ³⁄₁₆-in. shim, skirt, and top shim equals the width of the leg. The thickness of this shim should be around ¾ in. With the ³⁄₁₆-in. shim under the skirt and the leg butted up against them, measure the exact difference. The back shim cannot be wider than ⅝ in. though; otherwise, it would block the pocket screw holes (see the left photo above). To attach the skirt to the leg, lay both ³⁄₁₆-in. shims under the skirt and butt the leg up against it. Make sure the tops are flush, and secure the assembly to the bench with the face clamp. (With multiple shims and parts, this process can be a bit awkward.) When the face clamp is secured, check that the ends are still flush with

It's important that the inside of the joint between the leg and lower stretcher is flush. It can be tricky to cut a shim that is the perfect thickness, so I add a piece of card stock to increase the thickness if the shim alone is not doing the job.

With bar and face clamps holding the assembly, slowly drive the long screw through the lower stretcher and into the leg.

a straightedge and that the joint is tight. A bar clamp across the skirt and over the leg will help keep things stable while you drive the pocket screws. Repeat with the matching back leg to this side.

The lower side stretchers are 1⅜ in. thick and butt up against the 1¾-in. legs. Cut two ⅜-in. shims to elevate the side stretcher when using the face clamp. Place the leg assembly face down on the bench. With the skirt already installed, it will be a snug fit to slide the side stretcher into place; be careful not to force the legs too far apart when positioning. Align the stretcher so that the bottom is 3¾ in. up from the bottom of the leg (see the top right photo on p. 67). Position shims under the stretcher; use card stock if necessary so that the joint is perfectly flush. Double-check that the stretcher hasn't shifted from the 3¾-in. measurement, and clamp with the face clamp. Clamp across the legs with a bar clamp. Predrill ⅛ in. deep with a long drill bit and then slowly drive a 2-in. pocket screw. Repeat for the remaining screw. Continue this process with the shims and face clamp on the opposite side. After one side of the table has been assembled, start from the beginning and assemble the opposite side.

Installing the Front and Back Skirts

With both sides assembled, flush-sand the joint between the stretcher and leg. Check the results with a straightedge. The lower shelf will butt against the stretcher and legs, so if it's not flush, the reveal between the shelf and stretcher will not be even. Round over the corner of the leg

Flush-sand the butt joint between the leg and the stretcher after assembly.

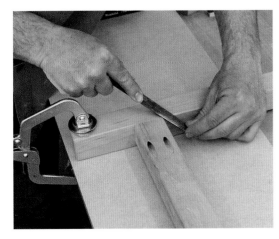

With the lower stretcher installed, finish the roundover on the leg above and below the stretcher.

above and below the stretcher on the inside edge with a file. Now, using the right-angle jig to hold one of the sides upright, position the front or back skirt, $\frac{3}{16}$-in. shim, and $\frac{3}{4}$-in. shim against the leg. Secure with the face clamp and bar clamp. Use a straightedge to check that the top of the leg and skirt are flush, then drive two pocket screws through the skirt. Remove the right-angle jig, and transfer the shims and remaining skirt to the other side. Clamp the skirt with the face clamp and bar clamp, and slowly drive two pocket screws. Clamp the right-angle jig to the remaining side assembly, and slide it against the skirt ends. With the shims secured with the face clamp, clamp across with a bar clamp. Check that the ends are flush, then drive two pocket screws. Move the clamps and shims to the other side and repeat.

Assembling the Shelf Supports

To complete the table base, install the lower shelf supports onto the side stretchers. These supports will be completely hidden from view. They sit $\frac{15}{16}$ in. below the top edge of the stretcher. Cut a shim to that width and another shim measuring $\frac{3}{16}$ in. by $\frac{5}{8}$ in., which will be needed underneath. The shelf support meets

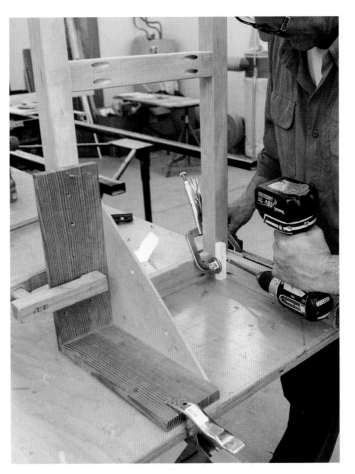

You'll need the right-angle jig to hold the sides upright during assembly.

With the face clamp holding the shims in place, drive pocket screws through the shelf support into the lower stretcher. A bar clamp across the support provides added security against slippage.

Hold the spacer frame joint in place with the face clamp while driving the pocket screws.

Clamp the batten to some heavy shop objects to help create a curve and to hold it in place while tracing the template.

Clean up the cut marks on the half template using a strip of wood wrapped with 80-grit sandpaper.

the side stretcher at the leg junction. Clamp it into position using the shims and face clamp. Drive two pocket screws through the shelf support, and repeat on the opposite end. Follow these steps to install the remaining shelf support to the lower stretcher.

Now you can assemble the ¾-in. spacer using the face clamp. Check that the ends are flush, and use a slow drill speed when driving the screws (see the top photo at left).

Cutting the Tabletop

The top has a slight curve on all four sides, which comes in ½ in. at the corners. To build a template that is symmetrical, I cut and shape a half curve on a scrap of ¼-in. medium-density fiberboard (MDF) and then use the half curve to make a symmetrical full-curve template.

Start with two strips of MDF 6 in. wide and 24 in. long. For the half template, measure over 7 in. and 16 in. along the long edge and make a mark. At the 7-in. mark, measure down ½ in. and draw a line. Next, cut a ⅛-in. by ¾-in. by 24-in.-long batten of knot-free wood. Clamp the batten to two heavy shop items like a handplane or a small vise, spacing them apart about 10 in. Align the batten at the 16-in. mark so that it is flush with the top of the template. At the 7-in.

Align the half template onto the full template, and trace half of the curve.

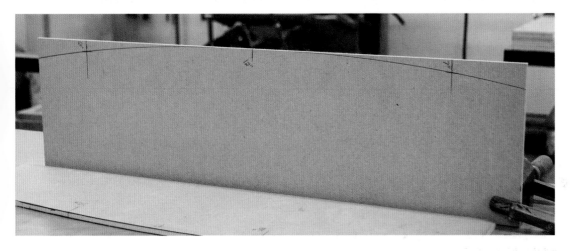

The finished curve is ready to cut.

mark, position the batten so that the face passes through the ½-in. line. Adjust the curve in or out by flexing the tail end. You want the curve to be flat in the middle but to increase its curve at the end. Trace the entire length of the batten. Cut the curve on a bandsaw.

Next, clamp the template upright on the bench. Take a thin scrap of wood at least 16 in. long, and wrap the strip in 80-grit sandpaper. Fair the curve by sanding along the length of the curve. To check if the curve is fair, roll it on the benchtop to feel for bumps.

Once the half template of the curve is done, you can make the full template. Take the other piece of 6-in. by 24-in. template stock, and make marks at 3 in., 12 in., and 21 in. With a square, make a ½-in. hash line at the 3-in. and 21-in.

Measure in ½ in. on both sides of the corner to mark the point that the curve will pass through.

Align the template on the tabletop so that the center and end marks correspond. Trace the outline onto the top.

marks. Clamp the two templates together so that the 7-in. mark from the half template lines up with the 3-in. mark on the full curve template. Trace the half curve onto the full template. Flip the half template, and line up the 7-in. mark with the 21-in. mark on the full template. Trace the curve, then cut out the full template. As before, use the 1-in. batten and 80-grit sandpaper to clean up the curve, and check for flat spots by rolling the curve on the benchtop.

Cut the top material at 18 in. square. Mark the center at 9 in. on each side, and at each corner make two ½-in. marks in both directions (see the bottom photo on p. 71). Set the full template on top of the 18-in. square, aligning the ½-in. marks with the marks at 3 in. and 21 in. on the template. Check that the 12-in. template mark matches the 9-in. halfway mark on the tabletop. Clamp at both ends and trace the template. Repeat on the three remaining sides.

WORK SMART

I cut the tabletop curve on the bandsaw and then use the template and a router to clean up the cut. In this case, I leave the line when cutting the curve and use the router to take the line. If you're not going to use a router, take the line when cutting on the bandsaw.

Use a router with a bearing in the middle to follow the template and clean up the sawmarks.

After the curves have been cut, reposition the template and clamp at both ends. Make sure the 12-in. and 9-in. marks are lined up. Use a ½-in. router bit with a bearing in the middle to follow the template and clean up the cut. Repeat on the three remaining sides.

Fitting the Shelf

The lower shelf slides in between the legs and lower stretchers. Since the shelf supports are supposed to be 12¾ in. wide, the shelf must be cut just slightly under this dimension so that it will slide into place without scratching the legs. I set the saw fence at 12¾ in. first and tested the cut on a scrap of plywood. It slid in without much fuss and had an even shadow line against the side stretchers. Confident that this fence setting was right, I cut the real shelf and slid it from the back into place to check the reveal. It's OK if the fit is not perfectly tight because the shelf sits below the top edge of the stretcher and a small gap isn't distracting. If the finished gap were not consistent, I would probably cut it so that an even ¹⁄₁₆-in. gap on either side of the shelf would hide the discrepancy. Rounding over the top edge lightly will help lessen any gaps. Finish-sand the tabletop and shelf, then oil all the parts.

Attaching the Top and Shelf

The top and lower shelf are attached to the table using pocket screws and #10 flat washers via a ¼-in. hole to allow for wood movement across the grain. Set the spacer frame with the pocket screw holes facing down on the bench. The 2-in.-wide frame pieces go along the sides. Starting from the front, measure down the side, making marks at 2¼ in., 7½ in., and 12¾ in. At each mark, measure in 1 in. to center the hole on the rail. Repeat on the opposite side. Drill the hole at the 7½-in. mark with a ⅛-in. drill bit. This allows the table to expand and

Slide the test shelf into place, making sure that the fit is not too tight and the shadow line between the shelf and the stretchers is consistent.

Drill oversize holes in the spacer frame to allow for wood movement of the top at the edges.

contract from the center attachment. The 2¼-in. and 12¾-in. marks are drilled with a ¼-in. bit, giving the pocket screw room to slide forward and back to allow for seasonal changes in the solid-wood top.

Next, drill out the lower shelf supports on the table. Drill a ¼-in. hole 1¼ in. from each end centered on the support. (One of my ¼-in. holes lined up directly above a pocket screw hole, so I was forced to use a bigger washer to span the pocket screw hole.)

Install the lower shelf, sliding it in from the back. Center the shelf on the table, and clamp it to the support rail at the front and back, using protective cauls against the finished surface of the shelf. Now tip the table on its side with a protective blanket underneath. Using the ¼-in. bit, barely touch the drill to the support rail to establish the center. Then predrill the hole using a ¹⁄₁₆-in. bit, being careful not to drill too deep. Take a pocket screw and #10 washer, and drive the screw by hand. Repeat on the remaining holes.

Clamp the shelf in place using protective cauls against the finished surface.

Attach the lower shelf with pocket screws and #10 washers. Drive the screws by hand to ensure the holes don't get stripped out.

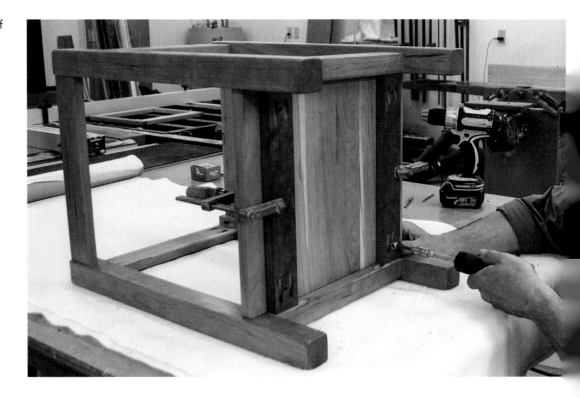

Mark the diagonals on the underside of the top to help locate the spacer frame, then use the diagonal marks and a square to center the frame on the top.

Attach the spacer frame to the tabletop with pocket screws and #10 washers, driving the screws by hand.

Use a square to center the base on the top before attaching it.

Predrill ⅛ in. deep first and then drive the pocket screws through the top of the legs into the spacer frame to install the top.

Next, mount the frame to the top. Because the top is curved on all four sides, it's a bit awkward to locate the frame. I used a straightedge to make marks along the diagonal at the corners to help center it. It's still necessary to measure the middle distance from the edge of the top to the frame to get it exact (see the top left photo on p. 75). When the frame is centered, make a few pencil lines on the inside to mark its location. Clamp the frame/top assembly to the bench, checking to make sure it didn't move. Predrill and screw the two center holes. On the outside holes, use a ¼-in. bit to locate the center of the hole, then predrill with a ¹⁄₁₆-in. bit. Drive the pocket screws with a #10 washer by hand (to

make sure they don't get stripped out or over-tightened).

Now you can set the table on the top assembly. Measure over from the edge of the legs to the frame to center the top. Clamp the table to the bench to secure it while drilling and screwing the corner holes. It's nice to have a long predrill for situations like this when you don't want the assembly to slip and it's hard to really get a good clamp on it to hold it steady. The long predrill doesn't go very deep; it just gives the screw a nice positive start. Slowly drive the pocket screws in all four corners, making sure that none go through the top!

DAYBED

6

Projects for my family usually fall under the category of need rather than want. The projects that challenge and excite me aren't necessarily stuff that we need. My wife is even less excited about a project that will take me months to complete. To convince her that I should make it instead of buying it from a retailer, I have to show that it can be done fast and be affordable, pleasing to look at, and functional. The challenge and excitement

MATERIALS

QUANTITY	PART	ACTUAL SIZE	CONSTRUCTION NOTES
END PANELS			
2	Top panel rails	⅞ in. × 2¾ in. × 39 in.	Maple
2	Bottom panel rails	⅞ in. × 3¾ in. × 39 in.	Maple
4	Corner posts	⅞ in. × 3¾ in. × 29¼ in.	Maple
2	Plywood panels	¾ in. × 39 in. × 22¾ in.	Maple plywood
2	Armrests	⅞ in. × 3¾ in. × 42¼ in.	Maple
2	Inside ply-panel	¾ in. × 8 in. × 39 in.	Maple plywood
2	Inside solid maple panel	¾ in. × 7½ in. × 39 in.	Maple
4	Furring strips	¾ in. × 1⅞ in. × 15¼ in.	Plywood
FRONT/BACK FACE FRAME			
2	Top face frame rails	¾ in. × 2¾ in. × 80 in.	Maple
1	Bottom face frame rail	¾ in. × 1⁷⁄₁₆ in. × 80 in.	Maple
2	Face frame stiles	¾ in. × 1½ in. × 11¾ in.	Maple
DRAWER BOX/MATTRESS SUPPORT			
1	Plywood top	¾ in. × 39 in. × 81½ in.	Maple plywood
4	Drawer partitions	¾ in. × 11¾ in. × 39 in.	Maple plywood
2	Drawer box support rails	¾ in. × 4¼ in. × 81½ in.	Maple plywood
2	Drawer slide shims	¾ in. × 1½ in. × 21 in.	Maple plywood
8	Floor spacers	¾ in. × 4¼ in. × 6 in.	Maple plywood
DRAWERS			
6	Drawer sides	¾ in. × 10⅞ in. × 21¹⁄₁₆ in.	Maple plywood
6	Drawer front/back	¾ in. × 10⅝ in. × 23¾ in.	Maple plywood
3	Drawer faces	¾ in. × 11⅝ in. × 25½ in.	Maple plywood
3	Drawer bottoms	¼ in. × 24½ in. × 20¹⁄₁₆ in.	Maple plywood

thus ends up being how quickly I can build something that I like.

A recent comment by my wife that our oldest son needed a new bed and that she was looking at some online caused me to utter those infamous words, "Why don't I just make him one? I'll do it simple, take me a weekend tops." Even though she knows that it will probably take a bit longer and cost a bit more, the fact that my goal is to do it fast and cheap convinces her that this is a good idea.

Designing the Daybed

So with the theme of speed and affordability, I begin the design process. Pocket screws will be a must, as they will allow the bed to go together quickly. And since I can hide all the screw holes, it will help keep the bed looking clean, with no visible fasteners unless you look really hard. Plywood will also be an integral part, as milling and sanding solid wood is time-consuming and expensive. But the finished bed needs to appear to be made out of solid wood and not sheet

DAYBED

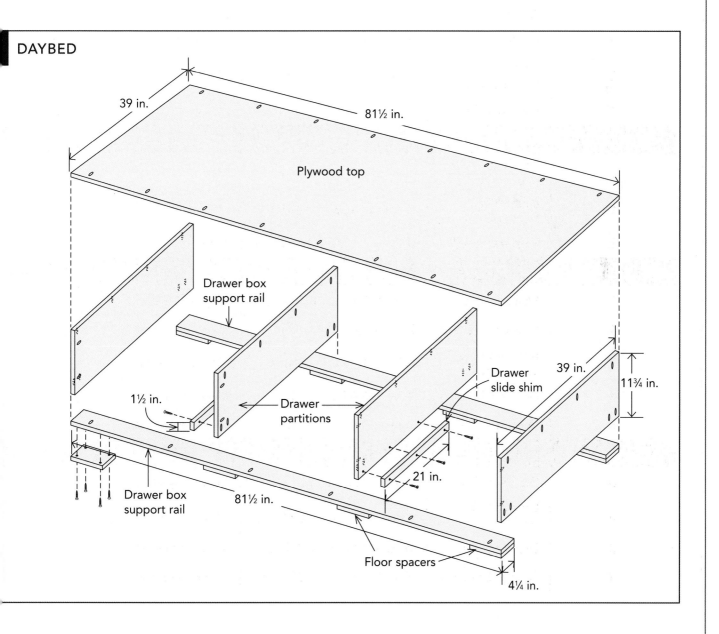

material. Also, since our son's room is pretty tight, adding some drawers underneath will be both functional and aesthetic. I decide on a daybed with armrests at either end instead of a headboard and footboard, giving the bed a lower profile for his already cramped quarters. Prefinished maple plywood for the drawer cabinet, end panels, drawers, and drawer fronts will mean no sanding and finishing for most of the surfaces. Solid maple for the corner posts, face frame, and armrests will give it a solid wood feel while concealing the plywood core.

A daybed covers a lot of territory: It's a bed, a couch, and a dresser all in one. Those are very different functions, so to combine all three under one label is something of a balancing act. To maximize the drawer space underneath, I decided on 11¾-in.-tall by 21¹⁄₁₆-in.-deep drawers, which allows me to get all the drawer sides and fronts from one sheet of plywood. In addition, 21-in.-deep drawer slides are the most common and thus affordable. These drawer dimensions coupled with an 8-in.-tall twin mattress give a comfortable sitting height of around 18 in. with the mattress compressed, similar to a dining room chair. For a more couchlike feel, a compressed mattress height of 12 in. to 14 in. would be better. The two end panels of the daybed are the same height. A 3¾-in. armrest caps the top and gives just enough room for a clock radio, small lamp, or phone.

Cutting the Parts

There are three main parts to this bed: the drawer cabinet, the end panels, and the drawers. Although for our family's uses the bed will always be up against a wall, there isn't any difference in construction between the front and back other than the fact that the wall-side face frame is composed of only the top face frame rail, which serves as a mattress border. I was able to get all the parts out of three full sheets of plywood and five somewhat wide solid maple planks 8 ft. long and ¹⁵⁄₁₆ in. thick. It's important

that the solid maple is ¹⁵⁄₁₆ in. thick because all the parts of the end panels are planed to ⅞ in. The face frame on the drawer box and the mattress support in back are ¾ in. thick.

CUTTING THE PLYWOOD PARTS

Set one of the sheets of plywood aside to be used for drawers, and rip an 8½-in. by 96-in. strip from each of the remaining two sheets. Set the nicer-looking strip aside to be used later on the end panel for the mattress to butt up against. The other 8½-in. strip will be ripped in half and used to support the bottom of the drawer cabinet. A tall twin mattress measures 39 in. by 80 in. (For some reason, purchased mattresses are a little smaller than their stated measurements, but you can use the measurements for construction purposes.) The drawer cabinet top mattress support, partitions, and plywood end panels all share this 39-in. width, so rip the two sheets of plywood to 39 in. wide. One sheet will be used as the drawer cabinet top; the other sheet will yield the end panels and drawer partitions.

The partitions are 11¾ in. tall and the end panels are 22¾ in. tall, which should yield an inch or so at either end of the plywood sheet to discard. Take your time laying out these cuts, and if possible cut the sheet in half to make it easier to manage on the saw. Once you've cut the end panels, label them and set them aside.

Since the end panels will be visible and the partitions will be hidden, make sure to lay out the cuts so that the best-looking veneers will be on the end panels and any irregularities or blemishes will be on the partitions.

PLYWOOD COMPONENTS

Sheet 1

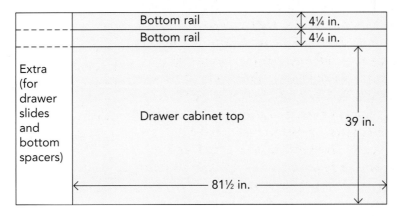

Sheet 2

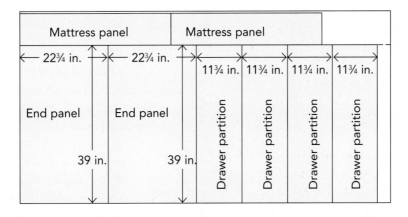

Sheet 3

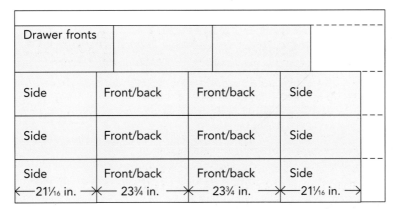

Label the four drawer partitions with a cabinet-maker's triangle to help you keep track of their order and orientation.

Drill pocket holes into the four drawer partitions using the benchtop jig.

Crosscut the drawer cabinet top and the bottom support rails to 81½ in. long. Set the leftover end piece aside to be used later for drawer slide shims and bottom spacers.

Drilling Drawer Partitions for Pocket Holes

With the four drawer partitions cut to 11¾ in. by 39 in., label them with a cabinetmaker's triangle. Then drill pocket holes in the partitions as shown in the drawing on p. 79. The two outside partitions get two holes on the inside faces on the vertical edges to attach the corner posts. The two middle partitions will have two holes on the inside edge at the front only for attaching the face frame. All four partitions get a row of pocket screw holes on

the top and two sets of two holes on the bottom at the front and back to attach the top panel and bottom rails. The end panels have these holes on their outside face; the inner panels have the holes on their inside face. There will be pocket screw holes on the top panel and bottom rails, too, but wait until the box is assembled and use the portable pocket screw jig to drill these.

Assembling the Drawer Cabinet

Assemble the drawer cabinet upside down on a set of sawhorses. Clamp and screw the outside partitions first, using the right-angle jig to help hold the partitions upright. The inner partitions will also have a ¾-in. by 1½-in. by 21-in. ply-

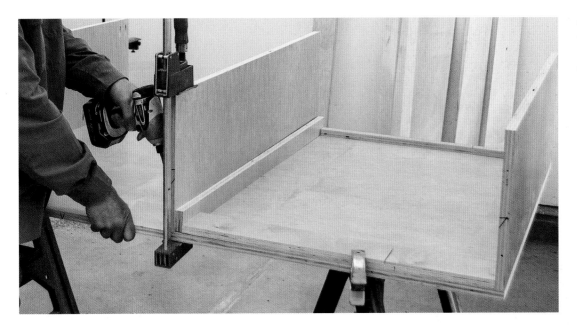

Use shims and clamps to properly locate the middle partitions when driving the screws.

wood strip screwed to their outside face. The combined 1½-in. width of the strip and partition makes it possible for the drawer slides to pass by the 1½-in. face frame. Take into account these two 1½-in. partition widths to calculate the area of the three drawer openings. For an 80-in. cabinet opening and the partitions described above, a 25¹¹⁄₁₆-in. spacer will yield three equal drawer openings. Cut two plywood scraps at 25¹¹⁄₁₆ in. to use as spacers. Use another plywood spacer that is at least 39 in. long to act as a stand-in drawer slide shim. Place the spacers against the cabinet end and the 39-in. shim against the spacers in the upright position. Align a middle partition against the shim and clamp into place.

To back up the screws, slide the shim as you work your way toward the back, screwing the partition to the top. Repeat on the other side. Measure the middle drawer width to double-check that you have three equal drawer openings. A slight difference of ¹⁄₁₆ in. will not matter.

INSTALLING THE RAILS AND DRAWER SLIDE SHIMS

Follow this same procedure to install the 4¼-in. bottom rails at the front and back. Install the

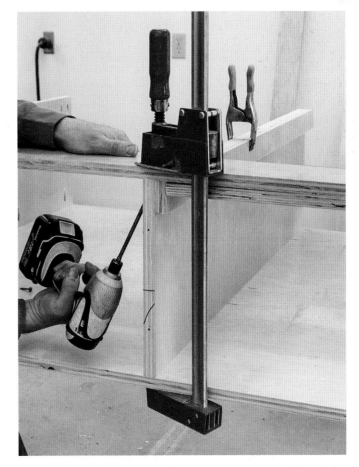

With the drawer cabinet upside down, hold the partition tight to the bottom support rail and drive the pocket screws.

Screw the drawer slide shim onto the partition with countersunk pocket screws.

¾-in. by 1½-in. by 21-in. drawer slide shims in the two outer drawer bays. Countersink with the stepped pocket hole drill bit to allow the pocket screw to sit below the surface and not impede the drawer slides.

The lower face frame on the drawer cabinet is 1½ in. wide, and you'll need to attach spacers to the lower rails so that the lower face frame is flush with the inside of the drawer box. Use the offcut from the large 39-in. by 81½-in. top panel

Adding spacers to the bottom support rails makes their combined thickness the same as the width of the lower face frame rail.

Clamp the top face frame rail into place, and use a square to transfer the location of the partition to the rail. This will mark the location of the face frame stiles. Do the same for the bottom face frame rail.

(or any available ¾-in. stock) to make these 6-in. by 4¼-in. spacers. You'll need to countersink the holes with the pocket screw drill to allow the pocket screws to sit below the surface. Round over the bottom edges of the spacers to keep them from scratching the floor or snagging on carpet.

Building the Face Frame

With the drawer cabinet constructed, it's time to obtain measurements for the face frame. The top and bottom rails are 80 in. long (the length of the mattress); they do not extend over the cabinet ends but stop short so that the corner posts of the end panels will cover the end partitions of the drawer box. The width of the bottom face frame rail can be no more than the actual combined width of the support rail and floor spacers, which is less than 1½ in. as per commercial plywood. A width of 1⁷⁄₁₆ in. is more realistic. The top face frame rail is 2¾ in. wide. Cut both the top and bottom face frame rails to length, clamp them centered on the cabinet, and transfer the partition locations to the rails. Check your measurements by stacking the two rails together and comparing the marks that were transferred from the drawer cabinet.

Drill a pocket hole on the top edge at both ends of the bottom face rail.

WORK SMART

Gluing the butt joint between the face frame stiles and rails does not improve strength, as the face frame is held securely and backed up by the drawer box, but it will prevent a slight ridge from ever forming at the joint.

END PANEL AND FACE FRAME

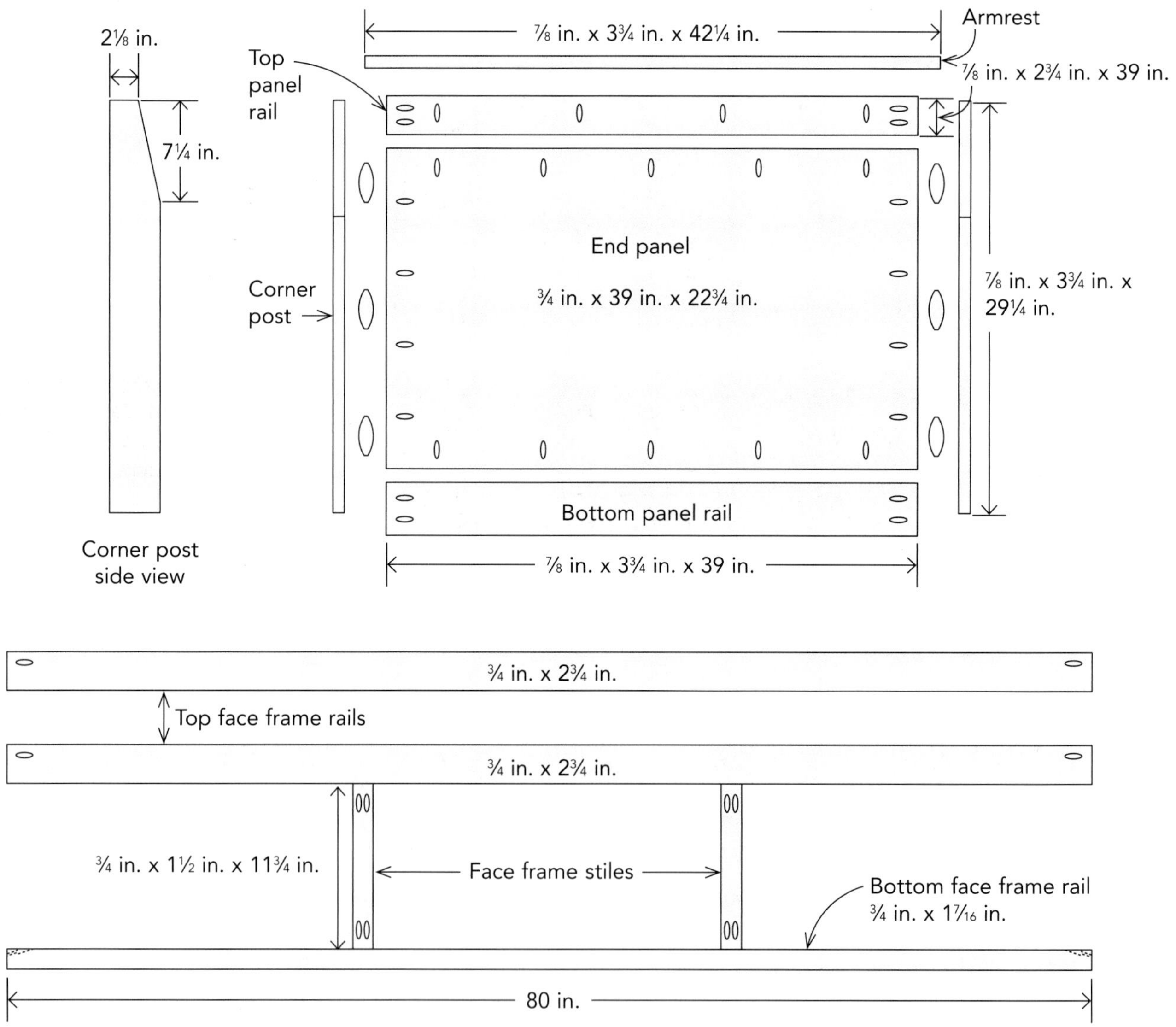

2⅛ in.
7¼ in.
Corner post side view
Top panel rail
Corner post
⅞ in. x 3¾ in. x 42¼ in.
Armrest
⅞ in. x 2¾ in. x 39 in.
End panel
¾ in. x 39 in. x 22¾ in.
⅞ in. x 3¾ in. x 29¼ in.
Bottom panel rail
⅞ in. x 3¾ in. x 39 in.
¾ in. x 2¾ in.
Top face frame rails
¾ in. x 2¾ in.
¾ in. x 1½ in. x 11¾ in.
Face frame stiles
Bottom face frame rail
¾ in. x 1⁷⁄₁₆ in.
80 in.

When screwing the stiles to the rail, it's easiest to orient the butt joint beyond the edge of the bench and clamp just the face frame with the face clamp.

Use a trim router (or a sander) to round over the edges of the face frame.

Mill two vertical face frame parts at ¾ in. by 1½ in. by 11¾ in., and drill two pocket screw holes on either end. The top face frame rail has a pocket screw hole at either end about ¾ in. down from the top on the inside edge (see the drawing on the facing page). The bottom face frame rail has a pocket screw hole at either end centered on the top edge. Drill these pocket holes before assembling the face frame.

Because the stile to rail joint is a butt joint that will later be sanded flush, you need to apply glue to the stile end grain. Hold the stile in the marked location on the bottom face rail with the face clamp and slowly drive the pocket screws. After the face frame is assembled, finish-sand and round over the edges with a router or sanding block.

Building the End Panels

Mill and cut the four maple corner posts as specified in "Materials" (see p. 78) and label them

Cut biscuit slots in the corner posts to help hold the plywood end panel in alignment during assembly.

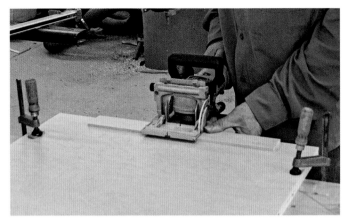

Use a ¼-in. shim with the biscuit joiner to create the step between the corner post and the end panel.

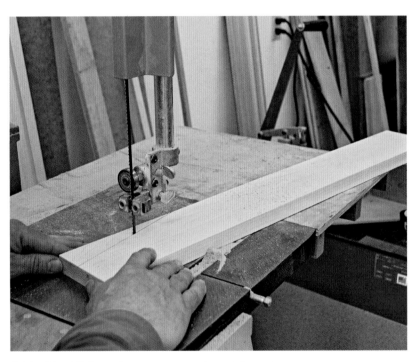

Add a bit of flair to the corner posts by cutting a taper.

The top and bottom end panel rails are pocket-screwed to the end panel, as are the front and back posts. I find it easier, however, to use biscuits in the end panels and corner posts during screw-up to help with alignment. There is a ¼-in. step between the outside edge of the corner post and the panel. Use one fence setting on the biscuit jointer and a ¼-in. shim to cut the biscuits on the corner posts and panels. Label the top and bottom of the panels and the inside edge of the corner posts to make sure you don't mess up and cut biscuit holes on the wrong sides.

After cutting the biscuit holes, draw the taper for the tops of the corner posts. On the front of the post at the top, measure over from the outside edge 2⅛ in. and make a mark. Then make a mark on the inside edge 7¼ in. down from the top. Connecting these two marks will give the taper of the post at the top. Cut the taper on the bandsaw and clean up the kerf.

The top panel rail gets a row of pocket screw holes on the inside top edge to attach the arm-rest and two pocket screw holes on either end to attach to the corner post. The bottom panel rail gets two pocket screw holes on either end to attach to the corner post. The panel gets pocket screw holes all along the inside perimeter to attach to the corner posts and rail; label the locations so you don't put a pocket screw where

front/back and right/left. Label the top toward the outside edge, as the inside edge will be cut at a taper. Cut the top and bottom end panel rails to length. These two rails need to match the plywood end panel width exactly; otherwise, there will be a gap when they are joined to the corner post. Measure each end panel individually because slight variances in the panel width should be expected.

there are biscuits. The top and bottom panel rails are ⅞ in. thick, so there is a ⅛-in. step between them and the end panel. Carefully round over the edges butting up against the panel—no more than ⅛ in. so as not to reveal a gap. Round over the edges on the corner posts next, again being careful to round it over no more than ⅛ in. A slight roundover with a sanding block, checking the results against the rail, will help keep track of how much wood you're removing. Finish-sand the corner posts and rails.

At this point, I apply finish coats to the rails, posts, and drawer cabinet face frames. I always prefer to prefinish my parts, but assembling and then finishing the entire project, especially if you're not using prefinished maple plywood, is also fine.

Since the frame material is not very wide, spraying lacquer with a spray can is a quick and easy option. Lacquer dries quickly and thus can be recoated soon after it dries. I use Deft® semi-gloss lacquer, which is widely available. Use outside or in a well-ventilated area. Sand in between coats with 320 or finer paper.

Building the Drawers

Constructing the drawers is next. Subtract ⁷⁄₁₆ in. from the opening to determine the drawer width. To save time, I didn't glue on solid-wood edge-banding and left the veneer core of the drawer box exposed. For a more finished look, glue on ⅛-in. edge-banding; plywood construction and edge-banding are covered in detail in

Use the right-angle jig to help with the drawer assembly.

the Vanity chapter (see p. 120). The drawer slides that you use will dictate the drawer part dimensions. If you use the Blum® Tandem slides for ¾-in. thickness, you'll get a drawer front and back length of 23¾ in. The drawer side height is 10⅞ in. with a length of 21¹⁄₁₆ in. The drawer front and back height is 10⅝ in. (¼ in. less than the sides). Cut the dado for the drawer bottom ½ in. up from the bottom edge. On the drawer backs, cut off the bottom ¾ in. so that the drawer bottom can be installed after the drawers are assembled. Drill for the drawer-slide locating pin on the back, and install the Blum mounting clips underneath at the front.

WORK SMART

Drawer slides come in models based on the drawer side thickness. Choose the model to be used for ¾-in. drawer sides; I used Blum Tandem soft-close slides for the daybed.

Clamp the bottom panel rail to the plywood end panel, and flush up the edge with a straightedge.

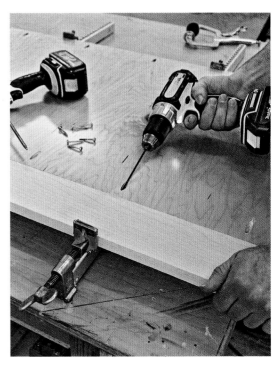

In the middle of the field, which is beyond the reach of the face clamp, use an extra-long predrill bit to get the hole started and to minimize shift.

Biscuits keep the joint from shifting so it's not necessary to use clamps in addition.

Assembling the End Panels

To assemble the end panels, first clamp the bottom panel rail to the plywood, using a straightedge to flush up the end joint. Use the face clamp and a ⅛-in. shim to keep the parts aligned for the first screw. In the middle of the field where the face clamp cannot reach, predrill

⅛ in. deep with an extra-long bit to minimize creep, or slightly offset the joint in the opposite direction (as explained in Chapter 1). Since there is a ⅛-in. step between the rail and the plywood face, a slight shift will not be noticeable, but learning how to reduce shift is a good habit to get into. Use a slow drill speed when driving the pocket screws. Repeat with the top rail. If the rail or panel is proud at the ends, use a plane or belt sander to flush them out.

Next, clamp the right-angle jig to the end panel in an upright position. Clamp the jig to the bench. Using the biscuits to align the corner post with the panel, clamp the assembly at the bottom to hold it in place. Check that the top of the post and the top panel are flush, and then drive a screw at the bottom. Where there are biscuits I don't feel that a clamp is necessary, but at the top panel rail I reposition the clamp and finish off screwing. Repeat the procedure with the remaining post.

Installing the Face Frame

Now we're ready to install the face frame. Flip the drawer cabinet upright on a flat bench, and drill pocket screw holes in the top panel and bottom rail with the portable pocket screw jig. I lay out the holes two per drawer opening. Hold the first and last screw hole about 5 in. from the ends. Repeat the pocket screw holes at the back of the cabinet on the top only.

Clamp the face frame to the drawer box starting with the drawer box support rail. Be sure to use clamp cauls to protect the surface. Measure over from the end of the cabinet on both sides to make sure the face frame is centered. Move your way along the bottom with clamps at each pocket screw location. For the top rail, clamp at both ends to hold the face frame in place and drive the first pocket screw. Work your way down the cabinet with hand pressure holding the frame in place. After the top is attached, screw through the middle partitions into the vertical face frame members.

INSTALLING THE DRAWER SLIDES

With the face frame attached, you can now install the drawer slides. Use a square to set the drawer slides back $^{15}/_{16}$ in. from the face. You'll need two scraps of plywood for the drawer slides to sit on at the back during installation.

The portable pocket screw jig is handy for very large panels that would be difficult to drill in the benchtop jig.

Attach the bottom face frame rail first, using clamps wherever there is a screw to hold it in place.

Use wide bar clamps to hold the top face frame rail to the plywood top.

Set the drawer slides in place, $^{15}/_{16}$ in. back from the face of the face frame.

A bar clamp at the end and some small scraps of wood clamped to the partitions help support the back face frame as you attach it to the drawer cabinet.

Use a try square set at ⅞ in. to mark the locations of the furring strips on the inside face of the corner posts.

To attach the top back face frame that will be against the wall, clamp small scraps of wood flush with the inside top of the cabinet to the partitions. These scraps will hold the piece in place while you clamp across the cabinet at either end. Use hand pressure against the frame piece while screwing in the middle.

Attaching the End Panels

Before the end panels can be attached to the drawer cabinet, you need to install furring strips on the inside of the corner posts. These strips will support the inside panels above the drawer cabinet. Lay the end panels face up on sawhorses. Apply a strip of blue tape on the upper portion to protect the maple posts when transferring the taper of the post to the furring strip. Measure up 14 in. from the bottom of the post to mark the top of the drawer cabinet location. With a try square set at ⅞ in., draw a line from the top of the corner post to the drawer cabinet mark (see the bottom photo at left). Measure from the back of the plywood panel to the line; the measurement should be about 1⅞ in. From the top of the post to the top of the drawer cabinet mark should be about 15¼ in.

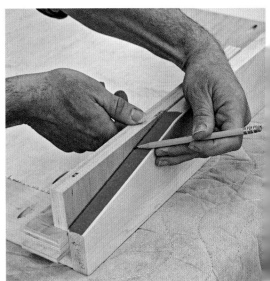

Raise the furring strip by about 1 in. to trace the slope of the corner post.

Clamp and attach the furring strips to the corner posts with pocket screws.

Cut four scraps of ¾-in. plywood at 1⅞ in. by 15¼ in. for the furring strips. To transfer the taper of the corner post, you'll need to raise the furring strips about 1 in. (I used scraps of ¾-in. and ¼-in. plywood underneath the furring strip on the inside). Cut the taper on the furring strip. Remove the shims and place the 1⅞-in. strip against the corner post, sliding it up until the taper on the furring strip meets the ⅞-in. pencil line on the inside of the post. Mark the location of the top of the post on the strip and trim off the excess. Place the strip back into position, and drive two pocket screws to hold it in place. Repeat on each post. The end panels are now ready to attach to the drawer cabinet.

The width of the plywood end panels and the depth of the drawer cabinet are both 39 in., so the corner post should slide right onto the cabinet. Chamfer the plywood edge of the drawer cabinet with a file to help the process. The face frame on the front of the cabinet will keep the end panel from sliding too far in when attaching with pocket screws. Drive two screws through the end partitions into the corner posts. Don't screw the face frame to the corner post just yet.

At the back of the cabinet, the top back face frame helps locate the end panel at the top of the drawer cabinet, but at the bottom there is nothing to butt against. Clamp a scrap piece of wood to the bottom rail of the drawer box to help keep it in place when attaching with screws

Clamp a scrap of wood to the drawer box support rail to help align the end panel when attaching it to the drawer box.

through the back of the end panel (see the photo above). With the drawer cabinet located to the end panels, you can now screw the face frame to the corner posts.

FINISHING THE INSIDE OF THE END PANELS

To hide all the pocket screw holes on the back of the panel, you need to do a bit of custom fitting. This is probably the most challenging part of the construction, so take your time. Two pieces fill in the gap in the end panel above the drawer cabinet. The first is about 8 in. tall (measure the distance from the top of the cabinet to where the furring strip starts to taper to be sure). This piece will mostly be hidden by the mattress. Use the 8½-in. by 96-in. strip taken

Slide the upper panel into place to test the fit of the bevel cut.

When the lower bevel on the solid maple inside panel is tight, mark the location of the top bevel.

from the plywood sheet (the one the end panels and drawer partitions were taken out of). Above this panel is solid maple board about 7½ in. tall with bevels cut on either side. Both pieces are held in place with glue and biscuits.

Starting with the lower panel, rip the plywood piece to 8 in. wide. Even though the cabinet and end panels are 39 in. wide, double-check the actual measurement. Measuring exactly and cutting some sample strips to test the fit will ensure that this highly visible butt joint will be tight. Cut and fit the lower plywood panels first, then the upper ¾-in. solid maple panels. To help the panels fit into place, round over the inside of the panel ends with a belt sander.

When both panels fit lengthwise, measure the bevel of the taper (in this case, 13 degrees). The bevel won't be seen at the top or back, so a perfect fit isn't necessary. Cut a sample bevel on a scrap to test the fit. Cut the lower bevel on the maple piece first and press-fit between the posts. Making sure that the lower plywood panel

is tight against the drawer cabinet and that the maple is tight against the plywood, transfer the line at the top of the corner post to mark the location of the bevel at the top of the maple panel.

Cut the top bevel. This will be partially hidden by the armrest, so it's better if it is slightly below the top of the post than slightly proud and misaligning the armrest. Next, cut a biscuit hole into the furring strip for both the lower and upper panels, being careful to avoid the screws holding the furring strip to the post. Transfer the biscuit hole marks to the back of the panels and cut them. Most likely the bevel cut on the maple board overhangs the plywood panel with a sharp edge. Soften this with a plane or sanding block, but don't cut too much off or you might see the plywood underneath. Leave this rounded edge slightly proud of the plywood face.

A Quick Fix for a Bowed Board

On one of the end panels, the fit between the plywood panel and the maple board was perfect; on the other, not so. The reason? The solid-wood board bowed in slightly so that when the bevel met the plywood, some of the veneer core was visible. To fix this problem, I screwed a short scrap of ¼-in. plywood to the back of the plywood panel, sticking up barely ³⁄₁₆ in. (see the photo at right). This keeps the two panels aligned and the veneer core hidden.

ATTACHING THE ARMRESTS

Before the panels can be glued into place, you need to attach the armrests. A matching 13-degree bevel is cut on the inside edge of each armrest. The armrest overhangs the corner post about ¼ in. on the inside and ¾ in. at the front and back. Because people will be tempted to move the daybed by grabbing it by the armrests, be sure that there are plenty of pocket screws holding them in place: Two at the front and back and two more in the field should be plenty. To attach the armrest, use clamps and protective cauls at the front and back to hold it in place.

GLUING THE INSIDE PANELS

Now the panels can be installed to hide all those pocket screw holes. Start with the lower panel, gluing the biscuit hole only on the furring strip and panel. Press the lower panel into place, making sure that it has contact with the top of the drawer cabinet. If the plywood is a bit twisted,

Attach the armrest to the end panel with pocket screws drilled up through the top end panel rail.

Apply glue to the biscuit holes in the furring strips and plywood panel.

The offcuts from the furring strips make great clamping cauls to hold the upper inside panel tight while the glue dries.

To save time, I chose not to edge-band the drawers or drawer fronts. If you go this route, it may be necessary to fill some gaps in the veneer core with filler on the top and sides of the drawers and drawer fronts. Also, a couple of coats of oil on the plywood edge will help keep it clean.

use a block of wood clamped to the mattress border to hold it in place. Repeat the procedure on the upper panel, gluing the biscuit holes only. Press the upper panel into place, using the offcuts from the furring strips as cauls. A strip of leather between the caul and panel will protect the surface.

Finishing the Drawers

Drawer fronts and handles are all that remain. Round over the back of the drawer front with a ¼-in. roundover bit, but on the front simply ease the edge over with a sanding block to keep the veneer core hidden.

Use drawer front locaters to help align the drawer fronts with an even reveal on all four sides (allow a ¹⁄₁₆-in. gap between the sides of the front and the face frame). Drill out the drawer front backs for the locating pins. With the locating pins pressed into the holes in the drawer front back, use ¹⁄₁₆-in. shims under the drawer front to mark the locations of the screws for the locaters. Drill out the holes in the drawers with a ³⁄₁₆-in. drill bit, and then pound the locaters into the drawer backs. Shift the drawer until the reveals are consistent, then tighten the screws. Drive pocket screws to finish installing the drawer fronts.

Installing drawer front locaters into the back of the drawer fronts makes it easy to achieve an easy reveal on all four sides.

The finished daybed is now ready to disassemble and move to its permanent location. You'll notice that not a single screw hole or putty mark is visible, which shows just how slick pocket joinery can be.

Installing the Bed

To install the daybed (or move it), you'll need some help. Remove the drawers and unscrew the end panels from the drawer cabinet. To accommodate uneven floors, place shims underneath the bottom rail of the drawer box. With the drawer box several inches from the wall, place the end panels back into position. Drive the pocket screws that were initially used in the shop to assemble the daybed, then slowly drive the remaining pocket screws from the face frame into the end panel.

This project shows how useful pocket screws can be when building face frames, plywood boxes, and cabinets that need to come apart to be moved or installed. My favorite application of pocket hole joinery on the daybed is the way the armrests are attached. To create such a strong joint that is completely hidden from view is what pocket hole joinery is all about.

With the daybed cabinet in place, attach the end panels via the pocket holes in the face frame.

Back or Backless?

There is no back on this drawer cabinet. If your daybed will be accessible from both sides, you'll need to add a back. Or better yet, have drawers coming out of both sides for added space. I chose not to have a back so that I could add drawers later if I wanted. Also, it makes removing the end panels easier, as you don't have to crawl into the drawer opening to access the back pocket screws. If anything falls between the wall and bed, you can access those things by removing a drawer instead of moving the cabinet/ bed. To add a back, screw furring strips on the sides and under the top mattress support.

7 BED

Pocket screws are like clamps and glue combined. They pull a joint together and hold it tight. Unfortunately, the one thing they don't do is align the joinery, as a mortise-and-tenon joint would. This has to be done with clamps and shims that hold the joint in place as the screws are driven. This process can be as simple as attaching face clamps and driving a screw or as difficult as holding multiple shims and clamping while trying not

MATERIALS

QUANTITY	PART	ACTUAL SIZE	CONSTRUCTION NOTES
2	Headboard posts	1¾ in. × 5¾ in. × 49 in.	Black walnut
2	Footboard posts	1¾ in. × 5¾ in. × 25 in.	Black walnut
2	Top rails	1⅜ in. × 5¾ in. × 52½ in.	Black walnut
2	Bottom rails	1⅜ in. × 5¾ in. × 52½ in.	Faced black walnut/alder
1	Bottom headboard rail	¾ in. × 5¾ in. × 52½ in.	Alder
2	Footboard stiles	1⁹⁄₁₆ in. × 5¾ in. × 7½ in.	Faced black walnut/alder
2	Headboard stiles	1⁹⁄₁₆ in. × 5¾ in. × 14¾ in.	Faced black walnut/alder
2	Footboard side panels	¾ in. × 6¹⁵⁄₁₆ in. × 7⁷⁄₁₆ in.	Oak plywood
1	Footboard center panel	¾ in. × 28¹⁵⁄₁₆ in. × 7⁷⁄₁₆ in.	Oak plywood
2	Headboard side panels	¾ in. × 6¹⁵⁄₁₆ in. × 14¹¹⁄₁₆ in.	Oak plywood
1	Headboard center panel	¾ in. × 28¹⁵⁄₁₆ in. × 14¹¹⁄₁₆ in.	Oak plywood
2	Lower mattress rails	⅞ in. × 5¾ in. × 80½ in.	Black walnut
2	Upper mattress rails	¾ in. × 4¾ in. × 80½ in.	Black walnut
2	Mattress support strips	⅞ in. × ¾ in. × 80⅜ in.	Alder
6	Mattress supports	⅞ in. × 4½ in. × 60⁷⁄₁₆ in.	Alder

to ding the work. Biscuits can provide some help in locating the parts to be assembled but only in one direction. A biscuited joint can still shift to either end of the slot. In addition, biscuits are wide and thus limit the width of stock they can be used on.

Enter the dowel. Two dowels can align a joint perfectly with little to no movement in any direction. Dowel holes run parallel to pocket holes, thus they can fit onto narrower stock and won't sacrifice the strength of the wood. Dowels are so good at aligning the joint that pocket screws can be driven without clamping across the joint. And dowels are readily available at hardware stores and are relatively cheap.

That said, you can build the bed without dowels using pocket screws alone. Using the face clamps and shim techniques described else-where in this book will guarantee strong con-struction. You'll need to take a bit more care during assembly to ensure proper alignment, but the design is still applicable to pocket hole

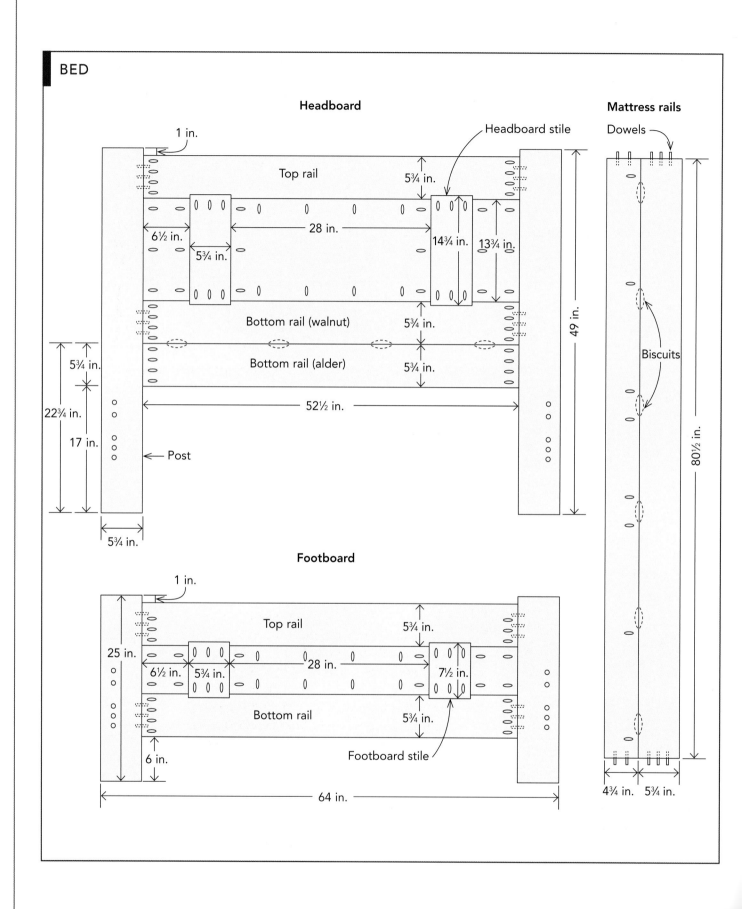

Headboard

1 in.

Headboard stile

Mattress rails

Dowels

Top rail

5¾ in.

6½ in.

28 in.

14¾ in. 13¾ in.

5¾ in.

49 in.

Bottom rail (walnut)

5¾ in.

Biscuits

Bottom rail (alder)

5¾ in.

5¾ in.

52½ in.

80½ in.

22¾ in.

17 in.

Post

5¾ in.

Footboard

1 in.

Top rail

5¾ in.

25 in.

6½ in. 5¾ in.

28 in.

7½ in.

Bottom rail

5¾ in.

Footboard stile

6 in.

64 in.

4¾ in. 5¾ in.

joinery. The one exception is the attachment of the mattress rails to the headboard and footboard; here, it's probably a good idea to use commercial bed hardware because pocket screws alone may not be strong enough and would make it difficult to disassemble and reassemble the bed for moving.

Design Considerations

The mattress height and bed location played a big role in the bed's dimensions. While the back of the headboard is completely hidden from view, the back of the footboard is not. Obviously any pocket holes in the footboard rail that are above the mattress height would be visible. I'm no less fond of plugged holes than I am of open holes, so I always try to keep them out of view. If the footboard were to extend above the mattress, for aesthetic reasons I would have eliminated the pocket holes in the footboard top rail and joined it with dowels and glue instead.

To determine the height of the footboard, I measured our mattress and box spring at a combined height of 18 in. The mattress has a pillow top that slopes down at the edges; the height at which the pillow top meets the mattress sides is 15¼ in. This last measurement determined the highest desirable location of a pocket screw hole on the footboard. To allow a little more room, I used three pocket holes instead of four on the top footboard rail (see the drawing on the facing page). The top pocket screw hole is 15 in. above the mattress supports. After the heights were determined, I positioned the short stiles on the footboard so that they formed a perfect square for the small oak panels on either side. On the headboard, the mattress top coincides with the center of the bottom black walnut rail.

I used 8/4 black walnut for the posts and rails, quartersawn white oak plywood for the panels, 4/4 black walnut for the mattress rails, and 4/4 alder for the mattress supports. Clear black walnut is really expensive and I wasn't particularly impressed with the lot of wood that

Dowels and pocket hole joinery work together to create strong, precise joints.

Facing the stock is a good way to stretch your material, but if you have enough wood on hand, there's no reason to add the extra work.

I was choosing from. To stretch my dollar and the clear material, I "faced" some of the stock. By facing, I mean gluing 4/4 black walnut to 4/4 alder to make boards that looked like 8/4 black walnut. This was possible on the bottom rails on both the headboard and footboard (where you couldn't see the top edge) and on the short stiles in the middle of the headboard and footboard.

Facing the Stock

To face the stock, mill the boards longer and wider than needed. For the lower rails and stiles,

When facing the wood for the stiles, drill for ¼-in. dowels through each end to help keep the material from slipping during glue-up.

Apply several clamps around the perimeter for plenty of holding strength as the glue dries.

boards 6 in. wide with about 2 in. of extra length will be oversize enough to yield 5¾-in.-wide stock. The extra length allows a ¼-in. or ⅜-in. dowel through either end to keep the stock aligned perfectly during glue-up. To index the mating pieces, clamp them together and drill for a dowel hole at each end. The dowel location is not critical, so there's no need to use a doweling jig here, but make sure that there is enough material between the dowel holes for the stock length. Using a foam roller, coat one of the surfaces with a generous amount of wood glue. Sandwich the pieces together and push the dowels in at both ends. Clamp around the perimeter of the piece. The boards will be cut to final dimension (after the glue has dried) at the same time as the headboard and footboard stock that isn't being faced.

Milling the Stock to Dimension

The posts, rails, and stiles are all 5¾ in. wide. Their thicknesses differ at each juncture to create a step. Between the posts and rails there's a ³⁄₁₆-in. step on the front and back. The short stiles protrude ³⁄₁₆ in. past the face of the rails in front to match the step of the post but are flush in back. Mill the stock for the headboard and footboard to dimension. Cut the posts and rails to length, but leave the short stiles long. Separate out the rails for the headboard and

Dado blades can create serious blowout at the back of the cut. Make sure to back up the workpiece with a scrap piece of Masonite® or other sheet material to prevent splintering. I used a pair of spring clamps to hold the Masonite in place.

footboard to notch for the short stiles. With eight identical dado notches to cut, it's well worth the time to set up a calibrated stop block.

CUTTING THE NOTCHES IN THE RAILS

The dado notch is 5¾ in. wide and ½ in. deep. Using a ½-in. dado blade stack, you'll need a 5¼-in.-wide block of wood for the stop block. The blade stack and block equal the width of the notch. Tuning the width of the notch takes some patience; testing the block size with the dado set installed on the tablesaw makes it difficult to fine-tune the width of the 5¼-in. block. (Two tablesaws would be handy in this situation.) I try to cut the block just a hair small so that the fit is too tight. Then I add pieces of blue tape to the block and test the notch width on a scrap of wood and a short stile. Sneaking up on the width with blue tape gives you control over a perfect fit. The final fit should be tight, since a small amount of wood will be removed with planing and sanding. With the block dialed in, I set the saw fence so that the final pass over the dado blade will cut the inside shoulder of the notch 12¼ in. from the end of the rail.

Set the distance from the stop block to the inside edge of the dado blade at 6½ in. Applying strips of tape to the stop block helps you micro-adjust the cut location.

Cut a test notch in a scrap of wood to check the fence setting.

Make the first pass over the dado blade with the stop block in place between the fence and the end of the rail.

Remove the stop block and cut the remainder of the notch, making multiple passes until you reach the saw fence.

Doweling Jigs

Doweling jigs are composed of a body that uses hardened drill guides of ¼-in. and ⅜-in. widths in conjunction with a fence and clamping mechanism to hold it to the work. Using a power drill and bit, you drill mating holes into two pieces of wood. Dowels

The Dowelmax jig comes with spacers and a locating pin. You can also make your own spacers to vary the distance from the outside edge of the workpiece to the center of the dowel hole. For long rows of dowels, an aluminum rod with adjustable ⅜-in. pin can be used to move the jig down the length of the workpiece.

are then inserted into the holes, and the joint is usually held together with glue. It's imperative that the drill bushings are perfectly aligned on the jig; otherwise, when the jig is flipped end for end when drilling alternate parts, any discrepancy will be doubled and the joint location will be offset.

Unfortunately, the more affordable doweling jigs available at hardware stores are not built to acceptable tolerances, so I would not recommend them for pocket hole joinery. I use a Dowelmax® jig. While it is expensive (at around $250 for the jig and ⅜-in. drill guides at most online outlets), it is built to such tight tolerances that I consider it a very good deal. The jig is quick and easy to use and highly intuitive. Using a series of shims, you can accommodate a wide variety of stock widths. I have used this jig extensively for more than 12 years and drilled thousands of holes with it and yet it still looks as good as new. Another jig you might consider is the JessEm™ doweling jig, which is also well made and a bit more affordable than the Dowelmax.

STEPPING THE RAILS

When all eight notches are finished, it's time to cut the rabbet in the rails and stiles for the plywood panels. For this, you'll need a rip blade on the tablesaw. With the scrap piece of wood used to set the notch width, set the rip blade height just a hair below the notch. Make sure that the rip blade does not score the notch. Set the saw fence at 1 in. With the rails 1⅜ in. thick and the fence set at 1 in. plus the saw kerf, a ¼-in. step

will be left between the front of the rails and the front of the plywood panels. With the faces out and backs against the fence, rip the shallow groove in the notch side of the rails and both sides of the stiles. Move the saw fence out of the way, then flip a short stile back side down, face up, and set the sawblade height so that it will remove the small strip of wood and leave a clean-cornered rabbet. Measure the exact distance from the top of the rail to the bottom of

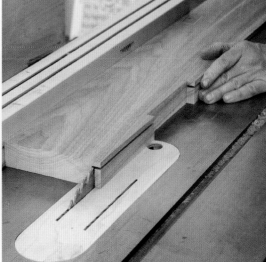

Make the first pass over the tablesaw to cut the rabbets in the rails and stiles (left). A second pass over the saw completes the rabbet cut (right).

the notch. Set the saw fence to a hair over this measurement. You do not want to remove any wood from the notch or the short stile will not seat correctly. Carefully remove the strip of wood from the rails and short stiles.

Adding the Dowels

The next step is to dowel the posts and rails. This will allow the headboard and footboard to be assembled in order to measure for the stile length. The Dowelmax jig (see the sidebar on the facing page) uses spacers between the fence and the bushing jig to allow for offsets between parts. There are spacers included with the Dowelmax, but it's simple to cut your own spacers to give you a wider range of options. I center the dowel holes roughly in the middle of the rail with a doweling jig spacer and then add a 3/16-in. clamping shim between the fence and spacer to allow the 3/16-in. step between the rail and the post. The top edge of the rail is 1 in. below the top of the post. I set the doweling jig 1 in. below

Use a try square to set the doweling jig position on the rail.

After drilling the first hole in the end of the rail, insert the dowel pin to make sure the jig does not shift.

the top edge of the rail and 2 in. below the top of the post. Three dowel holes are plenty to locate the rail. The dowels in this situation do not need to provide strength but are solely to help locate the rail during assembly. Leaving a space between dowel holes allows a spot to fit in a pocket hole.

To help me lay out the dowel and pocket holes, I used scraps from the posts and rails to do a small mock-up of the joinery detail. Once you're sure that no pocket holes or dowels will collide, drill all the dowel holes in the rails. Then, starting with the footboard posts, set the doweling jig 2 in. down from the top and drill for the dowels. The bottom rail is 6 in. up from the floor, so the jig must be set 7 in. up from the bottom of the post. Use a try square set at 7 in. to ensure that both posts have the doweling jig set at the same location. The posts on the headboard will also have the jig set 2 in. down from the top edge. The lower edge of the 1⅜-in. black walnut bottom rail is 22¾ in. up from the bot-

tom of the post; the doweling jig needs to be set 23¾ in. up from the bottom. The bottom alder rail (which will be finished with black walnut stain) will be installed with pocket screws only after the headboard has been assembled.

Joinery mock-ups with scrap play a vital role in pre-project planning. Here, a mock-up of a corner helps to visualize the design.

Mocking up the pocket hole locations helps to ensure that the holes won't collide.

It's important to carefully label which face the dowel fence will be against. Labeling with a pencil or scrap of blue tape really helps keep things in order.

To make sure that both posts are doweled identically, I cut a 23¾-in. scrap and clamped it to the post, flushing up the bottom edge with the bottoms to guarantee matching settings.

Dry-fit the headboard so you can measure the stile lengths and panel sizes.

Cut a scrap of wood to the stile measurement and test the fit.

Dry-Fitting the Headboard and Footboard

Before dry-fitting the headboard and footboard, clean up the notches with a file to make sure that there are no high spots. Assemble the footboard first with dowels. Measure the length of the short stiles. Use a scrap of wood to test the measurement; a press fit is preferred. Cut the stiles to length, and reassemble the footboard face down to measure for the white oak panel sizes. Cut the panels to the measured size (see "Materials" on p. 99). Repeat this procedure with the headboard.

Cut the stiles to length and check their fit. Then measure the panel dimensions from the back side of the headboard.

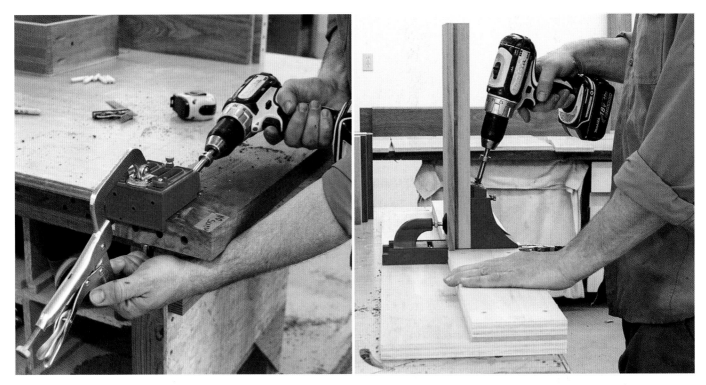

Use the portable pocket hole jig to drill the pocket holes in the rails (left). The stiles are short, so it's easier to use the benchtop jig for these (right).

Use the benchtop jig to drill holes in the plywood panels.

The short stiles are held in a notch, so dowels would be overkill. Drill three pocket holes for 1¼-in. pocket screws on the back of the stiles at this time. The rails for the headboard and the lower rail on the footboard get four pocket holes for 1¼-in. screws on the back side. The top rail on the footboard gets three holes; leave out the fourth top hole to ensure that it won't be visible.

The back sides of the plywood panels also get pocket holes. For the narrow panels, two pocket holes on the footboard panels and three on the headboard panels are plenty. On the larger center panel, drill pocket holes on all four sides spaced evenly throughout. I tend to drill more holes than I need, and during assembly it sometimes feels like overkill. But screws are relatively inexpensive and only take seconds to drive, so I don't mind erring on the side of caution.

(continued on p. 112

PLYWOOD PANELS

Headboard

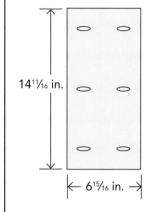
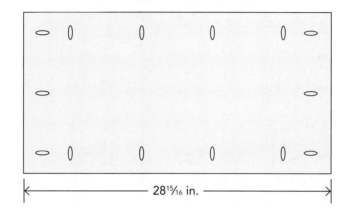

14$^{11}/_{16}$ in.

6$^{15}/_{16}$ in.

28$^{15}/_{16}$ in.

6$^{15}/_{16}$ in.

Footboard

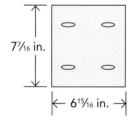
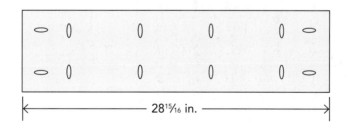
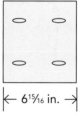

7$^{7}/_{16}$ in.

6$^{15}/_{16}$ in.

28$^{15}/_{16}$ in.

6$^{15}/_{16}$ in.

POCKET HOLE PATCH-UP

It happens: You drill a pocket hole on the wrong face and suddenly you're staring at an unsightly hole when you tried so hard to hide them all. Plugs are distracting in my opinion—the combination of the oval shape and end grain makes them stick out like a sore thumb. So when I drilled a pocket hole on the face of the mattress rail, my heart sank. **1** It was the last piece of walnut, and the inside face had several blemishes so I couldn't just swap it end for end.

If you make an honest attempt at patching a mistake, not just filling it with putty, I think most observers find it interesting instead of a flaw. I dug through the scrap bin and found a short piece of wood that came from the end of the board I misdrilled. Matching the grain is a good start in hiding the mistake. A clean rectangle patch seemed like the best approach. Using a ½-in. router bit, router, and short fence, I plunge-cut a ⅛-in.-deep mortise over the errant pocket hole. **2** From the scrap, I trimmed off a ½-in. by ⅛-in. strip matching the direction of the grain. **3** I held the long strip next to the mortise and tried to find a section that matched the grain pattern. Then I chiseled the mortise ends square and measured the patch length. **4** I used a handplane and shooting board to trim the ends so the fit was snug. **5** After applying a generous amount of glue, I tapped it into place with a mallet and small block of wood to keep the patch from breaking. **6** Granted, the dark grain of the black walnut helped to hide the repair. It would have been a different story had the wood been maple. **7**

Biscuits and pocket screws work together effectively when joining the two mattress support rails.

Assembling the Mattress Rails

The mattress rails are made up of two boards on each side. The lower board is ⅞ in. by 5¾ in. and the upper board is ¾ in. by 4¾ in. The lower board matches the width of the rail on the footboard. The dimensional step between the rails is a cosmetic detail that helps to simplify joining the two boards. Basically, it eliminates the need to flush-sand the boards along the edge joint. Mill two boards at ⅞ in. by 5¾ in. by 82 in. and two at ¾ in. by 4¾ in. by 82 in. Measure along the edges that will be joined, and mark for biscuits at 4 in., 16 in., and 32 in. from either end on both boards. Use the benchtop as a reference face with the backs of the rails down and cut

Insert the biscuits and tap the mattress rails together. There's no need to clamp the rails when driving the pocket screws because the biscuits will hold the boards in place.

slots for #20 biscuits. On the 4¾-in. rail, drill pocket holes to the sides of the biscuit slots. I drilled one hole before the first and second biscuit and one hole after the fifth and sixth biscuit. For the third and fourth center biscuits, I drilled a pocket hole on each side of the biscuit. Before joining the pairs of boards, finish-sand the outside surfaces.

With the outside surfaces of the mattress rails finish-sanded, you can join them with pocket screws. I used the right-angle jig to hold the lower rail upright. Slip in the biscuits and tap the rails together, making sure the ends are flush. After they are joined, cut the mattress rails at 80½ in., being careful to check that you won't hit a pocket screw when cutting.

I love the fact that I can construct every part of this bed with pocket screws and dowels—even the attachment of the mattress rails to the headboard and footboard. Here, the dowels provide the support and the screws keep the bed tight.

With the index pin set in the first pin of the doweling jig, drill for dowels in the third and fifth hole in the mattress rail.

Use the portable jig to drill the pocket holes in the end of the mattress rails. Dowels and four pocket holes will ensure a strong fit between the rails and the headboard and footboard.

When drilling the post for the dowels, use a 1-in. spacer in the doweling jig to align the mattress support rail location onto the post.

Cut biscuits in the bottom headboard rail and the alder rail. Pocket holes, biscuits, and dowels work together to ensure an accurate fit.

With the doweling jig fence referencing the inside face of the rail, set the jig 1 in. up from the bottom. Drill three ⅜-in. dowel holes, leaving a space in between them for pocket holes. To reset the doweling jig on the upper 4¾-in. portion of the mattress rail, push the index pin through the first hole of the jig into the last hole drilled on the support rail. This will ensure that the doweling jig is moved up the same amount on all four ends of the rails. Three dowels in the lower rail and two dowels in the upper plus four pocket holes spaced around the dowel holes will do the job.

The inside of the mattress rail is 1¾ in. from the outside edge of the bedpost. I reassembled the doweling jig to face-drill the post and used a 1-in. spacer between the jig and the fence. This can be confusing; take time to carefully mark which surface will be drilled for dowel holes. Better yet, drill a scrap of wood to represent the bedpost and check that the mattress rail lands in the right spot. I've found that misdrilled dowel holes can easily be fixed by gluing in a dowel, flush-cutting it off, and then redrilling. Set the doweling jig 7 in. up from the bottom of the post and drill holes.

A Second Bottom Rail for the Headboard

On the headboard underneath the bottom rail, I installed an alder board stained with Watco®'s dark walnut Danish oil. Adding the alder board ensures that there isn't a gap behind the mattress, and it's cheaper than using walnut in a hard-to-see area. Biscuit the alder board and bottom rail, measuring at 5 in. and 18 in. from both ends. The face of the lower walnut rail and the face of the alder rail will be flush. Drill pocket holes to the side of each biscuit slot on the alder rail and four pocket holes on each end. With all the bed parts cut to length and drilled for dowels and pocket holes, you can now finish-sand all the parts and apply coats of oil.

Assembling the Bed

To begin assembly, start with the footboard. Clamp the lower rail to the right angle jig, taping a 3/16-in. shim just below the dado notch so that the backs of the stile and rail are flush. Locate one of the stiles and hold with the face clamp. Drive a pocket screw under the clamp (see the top photo at right). Move the clamp to the other side and repeat. Finish attaching the stile by driving the middle screw. Repeat with the other stile. Then place the top rail on top of the stiles. Use the shim and face clamp to hold the top rail in place while you drive a screw (see the photo below). Continue clamping and screwing until the rail is secured. Lay the rail assembly face down on a protective blanket, insert the dowels, and slide the post into place (as shown in the middle photo at right) .

Use the right-angle jig to hold the assembly upright as you drive pocket screws through the stiles into the rails.

Slide the post into position on the rails, pushing the dowels into the holes.

Set the top rail into position, with the 3/16-in. shim in place. Attach the face clamp and drive pocket screws through the stile into the rail.

Using hand pressure against the post, drive the pocket screws.

When installing the white oak plywood panels, drive the pocket screws between the panel and post first to ensure a tight joint.

There's no need to clamp with dowels, but use hand pressure to keep the first screw from pushing the joint apart. Drive the remaining screws and repeat on the opposite post.

Now it's time to install the white oak panels in the footboard. Begin with one of the side panels. Because the seam between the bedpost and the small panel is not hidden by a rabbet, it will be screwed first to ensure that it is tight. Screw into the stile next, then repeat on the opposite side. Finish off by screwing the center panel into place.

ASSEMBLING THE HEADBOARD

Assembling the headboard rails and stiles is almost the same as the footboard, the only difference being that there's the additional lower alder rail to install. After attaching one of the

Screw the pocket screws from the panel into the stile.

Drive the pocket screws from the center panel into the stiles and rails.

Slide the lower alder rail into place before attaching the second post, and then attach the second post to the headboard assembly, starting at the top.

After the posts have been attached, drive pocket screws from the alder rail into the bottom headboard rail.

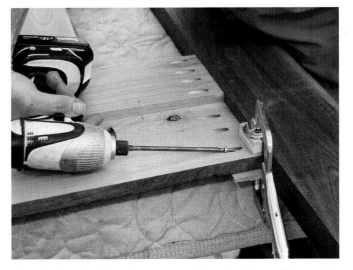

Use shims and a face clamp to position the alder rail onto the posts; drive the pocket screws.

posts to the rails, slide the lower alder rail into place with biscuits, double-checking that the end of the alder rail is not proud of the lower walnut rail. Locate the opposite post with dowels and then secure with pocket screws. Secure the alder rail to the black walnut rail with pocket screws. Using a ³⁄₁₆-in. shim in front of the alder rail and a ¾-in. shim in back, hold the assembly in place with a face clamp. Drive pocket screws through the alder rail into the bedposts.

Installing the plywood panels on the headboard is the same as on the footboard. The top and bottom pocket holes on the post side are close enough to the rabbets in the rails not to

Add the support strips to the inside of the mattress rails with countersunk pocket screws.

A block of wood helps to support the mattress rail as you attach the other end to the headboard.

bow when screwing, but the center one might shift a hair. Drive both the top and bottom holes first, predrill with the long drill bit 1/8 in. deep to start the hole, and then drive a pocket screw.

ADDING THE MATTRESS SUPPORT STRIPS

On the inside face of the mattress rails, flush with the bottom edge, is a 7/8-in. by 3/4-in. alder strip. This strip supports the alder boards that hold up the box spring. Cut the narrow alder strip 80 3/8 in. long. In order to use pocket screws to hold the strip to the mattress rail, you need to drill a 1/4-in. countersink hole. Measuring from each end of the strips, mark 3 in., 12 in., 24 in., and 36 in. for a hole. Countersink using a drill press or the pocket hole drill bit and collar. Hold the alder strip in place with the face clamp when attaching with screws.

FINAL ASSEMBLY

To assemble the bed, lean the headboard against the wall. Cut a couple of wide scraps of wood 6 in. long. I put a clamp at the bottom of the scrap to serve as an outrigger to keep the scrap from tipping over (see the bottom photo at left). With the dowels in the end of the mattress rail, slide it into place on the headboard. Set the opposite end on the 6-in. scrap of wood, and drive one pocket screw in the middle to hold it in place. Repeat with the other mattress rail. Place dowels in the ends of both rails, and slide the footboard into place. Remove the 6-in. scraps, and drive one pocket screw into each post on the footboard. Drive the remaining pocket screws into the posts. Place the six alder mattress supports on the thin alder strips and the bed is done.

Supporting the mattress rails with a pair of wood blocks makes it possible to assemble the footboard solo.

The finished bed . . . and not a pocket hole visible!

8 BATHROOM VANITY

Face-frame construction is by far the best application of pocket hole joinery. Considering your other options—dowels, mortise and tenon, or face-nailing butt joints—pocket screws are quicker, stronger, and easier. The strength provided by the flat-head screws driven at an angle guarantees that the only way the wood will come apart is if it is broken apart by force. The speed and accuracy due to the strength of the face clamp are unmatched.

MATERIALS

QUANTITY	PART	ACTUAL SIZE	CONSTRUCTION NOTES
PLYWOOD BOX			
1	Bottom panel	¾ in. × 19¾ in. × 47 in.	Maple plywood
4	Cabinet partitions	¾ in. × 19¾ in. × 28½ in.	Maple plywood
2	Top panel rails	¾ in. × 3½ in. × 47 in.	Maple plywood
4	Top panel stretchers	¾ in. × 3½ in. × 12¾ in.	Maple plywood
4	Drawer partitions	¾ in. × 3½ in. × 10½ in.	Maple plywood
1	Sink partition	¾ in. × 3½ in. × 23 in.	Maple plywood (wait to cut to final length until cabinet is assembled)
1	Back	¼ in. × 30 in. × 47 in.	Melamine
FACE FRAME			
3	Front stiles	⅞ in. × 1½ in. × 30 in.	Cherry
1	Front face corner post	⅞ in. × 1⅝ in × 30 in.	Cherry (corner post to be assembled from two pieces with a 45-degree bevel cut along the edge)
1	Side face corner post	⅞ in. × 3 in. × 30 in.	Cherry
1	Side back post	⅞ in. × 3 in. × 30 in.	Cherry
8	Horizontal drawer dividers	¾ in. × ¾ in. × 10½ in.	Cherry
3	Sink horizontal dividers	¾ in. × ¾ in. × 21½ in.	Cherry
2	Side panel rails	¾ in. × 3 in. × 15¹⁄₁₆ in.	Cherry (wait until side cabinet is assembled to make final measurement)
1	End panel	¼ in. × 15⁹⁄₁₆ in. × 24½ in.	A1 cherry plywood
2	Drawer fronts	¾ in. × 5⅛ in. × 10⅜ in.	Cherry
2	Drawer fronts	¾ in. × 6⅜ in. × 10⅜ in.	Cherry
1	Drawer front	¾ in. × 7⅞ in. × 10⅜ in.	Cherry
1	Drawer front	¾ in. × 5⅛ in. × 21⅜ in.	Cherry

MATERIALS

QUANTITY	PART	ACTUAL SIZE	CONSTRUCTION NOTES
DOORS			
2	Center stiles	¾ in. × 1¾ in. × 21⅜ in.	Cherry
4	Stiles	¾ in. × 2¼ in. × 21⅜ in.	Cherry
4	Under-sink rails	⅝ in. × 2¼ in. × 6⅝ in.	Cherry
2	Pull-out garbage door rails	⅝ in. × 2¼ in. × 5⅞ in.	Cherry
2	Under-sink door panels	¼ in. × 7⅛ in. × 18⅜ in.	A1 cherry plywood
1	Pull-out garbage door panel	¼ in. × 6⅜ in. × 18⅜ in.	A1 cherry plywood
DRAWER BOXES (WITH ⅛-IN. EDGE-BANDING APPLIED)			
4	Drawer sides, top row	¾ in. × 4⅜ in. × 18¹⁄₁₆ in.	Maple plywood
4	Sides, 2nd and 3rd row	¾ in. × 5⅝ in. × 18¹⁄₁₆ in.	Maple plywood
2	Sides, bottom row	¾ in. × 7⅛ in. × 18¹⁄₁₆ in.	Maple plywood
2	Top drawer fronts	¾ in. × 4¼ in. × 8⁹⁄₁₆ in.	Maple plywood
2	Top drawer fronts	¾ in. × 3½ in. × 8⁹⁄₁₆ in.	Maple plywood
2	Fronts, 2nd and 3rd row	¾ in. × 5½ in. × 8⁹⁄₁₆ in.	Maple plywood
2	Backs, 2nd and 3rd row	¾ in. × 4¾ in. × 8⁹⁄₁₆ in.	Maple plywood
1	Bottom drawer front	¾ in. × 7 in. × 8⁹⁄₁₆ in.	Maple plywood
1	Bottom drawer back	¾ in. × 6¼ in. × 8⁹⁄₁₆ in.	Maple plywood
5	Drawer bottoms	¼ in. × 9¹⁄₁₆ in. × 17½ in.	Maple plywood
VANITY BASE			
8	Short stretchers	¾ in. × 4 in. × 15½ in.	Maple plywood
2	Front and back	¾ in. × 4 in. × 47 in.	Maple plywood
1	Cherry face of base (front)	¼ in. × 4 in. × 48 in.	A1 cherry plywood (cut to exact length after installation)
1	Cherry face of base (end)	¼ in. × 4 in. × 17½ in.	A1 cherry plywood (cut to exact length after installation)

QUANTITY	PART	ACTUAL SIZE	CONSTRUCTION NOTES
HARDWARE			
5	Drawer slides	Blum Tandem plus 562F full-extension, for cabinets with a depth of 21 in.	
1	Under-sink tip-out tray with hinges		
1	Pull-out garbage can and drawer slides with door-mounting kit		

VANITY: FACE FRAME

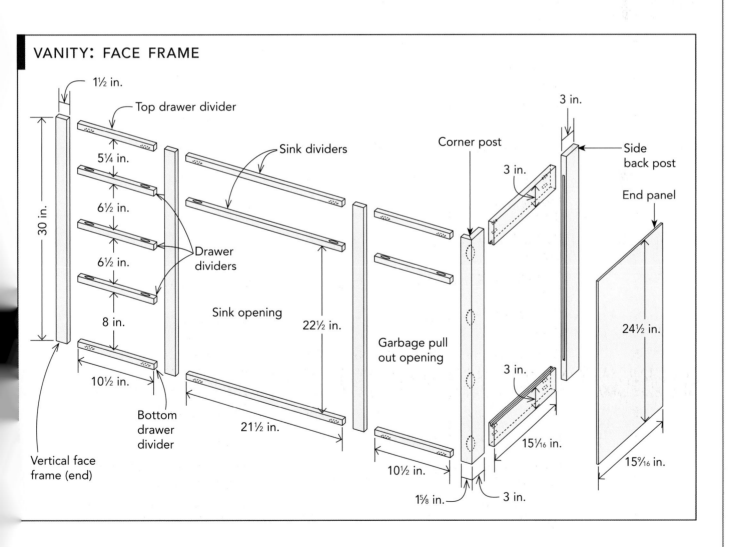

1½ in.

Top drawer divider

5¼ in.

6½ in.

6½ in.

8 in.

30 in.

10½ in.

Bottom drawer divider

Vertical face frame (end)

Drawer dividers

Sink dividers

Sink opening

21½ in.

22½ in.

Garbage pull out opening

10½ in.

Corner post

3 in.

1⅝ in.

3 in.

3 in.

3 in.

15¹⁄₁₆ in.

Side back post

End panel

24½ in.

15⁹⁄₁₆ in.

A bathroom vanity is particularly well suited for pocket hole construction because two of the sides are often against a wall, which makes it easy to hide the pocket screws used for assembly. A flush-front face frame gives the vanity a bit more class than is usual for a bathroom, and pocket screws make the process easy to accomplish. Pocket screws do leave a rather large hole, even with plugs, and for this reason they are sometimes avoided for door construction. But doors on a bathroom vanity don't receive the same scrutiny as a buffet cabinet and thus are great candidates for pocket screws. Drawers are always an excellent opportunity to use pocket screws because the holes are completely hidden by the drawer front.

The vanity described in this chapter is 48⅝ in. long, 21 in. deep, and 34 in. tall without the counter. The box is 30 in. tall and sits on a 4-in.-tall toe kick. The sink is centered on the cabinet with a row of drawers against the wall on the left and a pull-out garbage container and drawer on the right. The right side of the cabinet is exposed with a finished panel. Pocket screws are used in the construction of the plywood box, face frame, drawers, toe kick, doors, and cabinet end panel.

Making a Story Stick

To lay out the parts (and eliminate marking errors and miscalculations), it's helpful to make a story stick that shows the exact location of all the partitions and frame parts. A story stick also helps you locate pocket screw holes so that they don't land in the wrong spot.

Take a long scrap of plywood and lay out the horizontal measurements on one side. Flip the scrap over, and lay out the vertical measurements on the other side.

Laying Out the Parts

Using the solid-wood cut list, lay out the cuts for the doors, drawer fronts, end panel, and face frame on the solid ¹⁵⁄₁₆-in. cherry wood. Rather than cutting to the finished dimensions, it's a good idea to add ³⁄₁₆ in. or so to the initial cut widths to allow for wood movement like bowing and cupping. Begin with the drawer fronts and side-panel frame pieces since they are the biggest. For the front corner post, look for a 5¼-in.-wide piece with nice straight grain; the post will be cut and reglued with a 45-degree bevel to resemble a thick-looking corner post. You'll also need straight grain for the door frame members. Finish by laying out the three vertical ⅞-in. by 1½-in. and four horizontal ¾-in. by ¾-in. horizontal frame parts from the remaining wood.

Stock Preparation

Start with three ⅞-in. by 1½-in. by 31-in. and four ¾-in. by ¾-in. by 48-in. frame members. Cut these pieces out of the solid stock and mill them to dimension. Label one of the 1½-in. vertical frames "end"; this piece will go against the wall. Cut a ⅜-in. by ⅜-in. rabbet out of the back edge to make scribing it a little easier, as there is less wood to remove to accommodate any irregularities in the wall. Next, remove all of the machine marks on the faces with a handplane and/or sander. The inside edges should be cleaned up, too, but be careful on the 1½-in. vertical frames not to sand the edges out of square; otherwise, there will be a slight gap where the ¾-in. stock butts against them.

Finish by rounding over the front edges on all the pieces, using a block plane or sanding pad. Again, be careful not to over-round the 1½-in. frame members since the ¾-in. pieces must butt up against the edge. Use a sanding block with 120-grit sandpaper to control the roundover, and check it against a ¾-in.-thick scrap of wood. This won't be an issue on the ¾-in. by ¾-in. pieces because they won't have anything butting into their sides. The last sanding detail is to round over the front bottom edge of the vertical 1½-in. frame members; when this is done, these pieces will be ready for prefinishing. By starting the oil coats now, the frame members should be ready just as you are done assembling the box.

Cut a rabbet in the back edge of the vertical frame member that butts against the wall so that it is easier to scribe during installation.

Check the roundover edges by butting a ¾-in. frame against the 1½-in. frame.

Prefinishing the Parts

Whenever possible, I like to prefinish parts before assembly. For the vanity, the face frame, doors, and end panel can all be prefinished, as the vertical frame pieces are thicker than the horizontal frame parts, which means there's no need to flush-sand after assembly.

Prefinishing is a skill like anything else. It can be tricky to keep from damaging the pieces during assembly, but with some nice leather clamp cauls and a little extra care, you can get good results. At a minimum, apply two or three coats and save the last coat for after the parts are assembled, allowing cleanup of any nicks that might have occurred.

Apply oil to the parts in long, even passes using a wad of gauze wrapped in a scrap of a T-shirt.

Use the story stick to help lay out the pocket holes in the front web-frame piece.

I apply four coats of Daly's ProFin satin finish with a wad of gauze wrapped in a T-shirt scrap. I apply a light coat of finish with the grain and do not wipe off the excess. Sand with 220 grit after the first coat, followed by 320 or 400 grit after subsequent coats. Make sure to vacuum and wipe off with a rag all of the surfaces. There's no need to apply finish to edges that won't be seen. If there are any dust nibs after the fourth coat, I lightly knock them down with 1,000- or 1,500-grit automotive sandpaper. If you don't have a dust-free room for these pieces to dry while you're working on the box, wait until the end of the day to apply the oil coat and let it dry overnight.

I use prefinished maple plywood for the box. This is something your local lumberyard might not carry but will be able to order as it is quite prevalent in the cabinetmaking industry. Another affordable option that does not require finish is melamine. If you have to use unfinished plywood, you can prefinish it at the same time you're finishing the front-face frame pieces. Using the plywood box cut list, cut all the pieces to length and width, leaving the sink partition a bit long until after the cabinet is built.

Drilling the Pocket Holes

Begin by separating out the top panel web-frame pieces. Drill the pocket screw holes on the four 3½-in. by 12¾-in. by ¾-in. pieces (the stretchers) with two holes on each end (see the drawing on the facing page). Take the 3½-in. by 47-in. front web-frame piece (the rail) and mark the location of the pocket screw holes on the top, using the story stick to ensure that the pocket holes line up correctly. The exact location of the holes isn't critical, but make sure that they don't collide with the partitions. To hold the horizontal face frame pieces to the web frame, two holes for the drawer box opening and three holes for the sink opening are plenty. Mark the pocket screw holes about 3 in. from where each of the frame pieces starts and ends. After the holes are drilled, the web frame can be assembled.

VANITY: PLYWOOD COMPONENTS

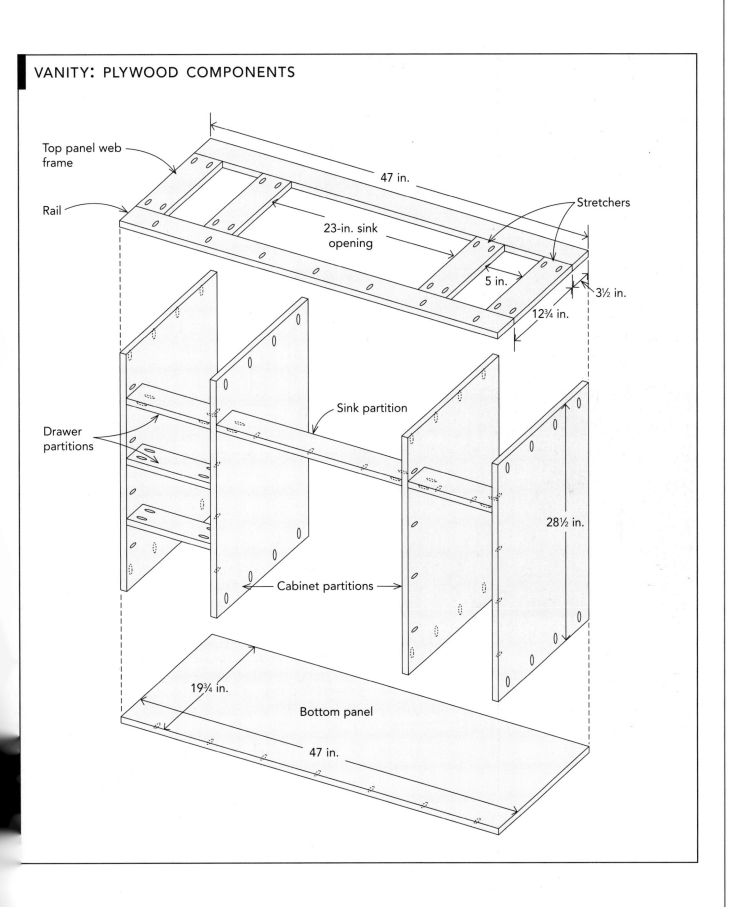

Top panel web frame

Rail

47 in.

Stretchers

23-in. sink opening

5 in.

3½ in.

12¾ in.

Drawer partitions

Sink partition

28½ in.

Cabinet partitions

19¾ in.

Bottom panel

47 in.

Use the face clamp to hold the web-frame parts together when driving the pocket screws.

Lay the plywood partitions on top of each other, and draw the cabinet-maker's triangle on the front edge.

WORK SMART

When laying out the pocket screw holes on the partitions and cabinet bottom, avoid putting them where a drawer slide will go or where they might be blocked by a drawer divider.

ASSEMBLING THE WEB FRAME

To assemble the web frame, start with one corner hanging over the edge of your bench, flush up the ends, and apply the face clamp. Screw the joint together and repeat on the opposite corner. Continue in this manner until the outside edge of the frame is assembled, and then place the interior web-frame pieces inside the frame, located 12 in. over from the outside edge (use the face clamp and the right-angle jig to help in assembly). This cabinet has a sink that requires a 23-in. rough opening, which dictated the location of the cabinet partitions and web frame.

Prepping the Plywood Partitions

Next, stack the four plywood partitions on top of each other and flush up the front edge and ends. Check to see that they are all the same length and square to each other. Label the front edges with the cabinetmaker's triangle. The location of the pocket screw holes is based on two things: being able to hide the screw holes and the ease of location for assembly. Given that this is a bathroom vanity and won't receive the same scrutiny as a china cabinet, I will try to limit the screw holes visible under the sink, but the drawer boxes and garbage pullout will be fair game. Also, I want to use the drawer partitions as a jig to locate the middle cabinet partitions, so I'll want to drill those holes on the opposite side of the drawer box. This will make assembly easier as the screws will pull the cabinet partitions tight against the drawer partitions, ensuring that the 10½-in. width will not vary. For a detailed guide to locating the pocket screw holes, see the drawing on p. 127.

Locate the pocket screw holes on the partitions and the cabinet bottom with a pencil and the help of the story stick. On the bottom of the cabinet, I locate the screw holes on the underside, which keeps them from filling with debris and also makes it easier to attach the face frame by screwing from the outside.

ASSEMBLING THE BOX

Once the pocket screw holes have been drilled on the partitions and cabinet bottom, you can begin to assemble the box. The right-angle jig acts like a third hand when clamping the cabinet pieces together. By clamping the jig to the bottom panel, you can keep it upright while positioning the end panel and clamping it in place (see the photo at right). Flush up the front ends and place a clamp along the top edge. Place another clamp just below the first pocket screw hole and drive in a pocket screw.

Continue lowering your clamp just below each pocket screw hole until you are at the bottom. Use the right-angle jig to hold up the opposite cabinet end and pocket-screw it into place. Clamp the top web frame onto the cabinet ends and attach with pocket screws.

Use the right-angle jig to help support the plywood pieces when attaching the clamps.

Clamps at each screw hole help ensure that the parts do not shift during assembly.

Counteracting Shift

When assembling the cabinet, since the direction of the screw is at an angle, it tends to pull the pieces in that direction. This movement doesn't happen when using face clamps because there is pressure on both sides, but in this case there is nothing to keep the pieces from creeping in just a bit. This is the major complaint with pocket screws (see p. 9), and it usually occurs in this particular situation.

There are two ways to counteract this shift, or creep. One is to use a very low drill speed; the other is to anticipate the shift by aligning the cabinet parts $\frac{1}{64}$ in. in the opposite direction that the screw will pull. If the cabinet part doesn't shift but you allowed for it by offsetting the pieces $\frac{1}{64}$ in., simply tap it into place with a mallet. This combination of drill speed and anticipating the shift will make it easy to match up the cabinet parts perfectly.

Set (but don't screw) the horizontal drawer partitions in the cabinet to help locate the vertical interior cabinet partitions.

With the short drawer partitions backing up the panel, screw the vertical partition to the bottom panel of the cabinet.

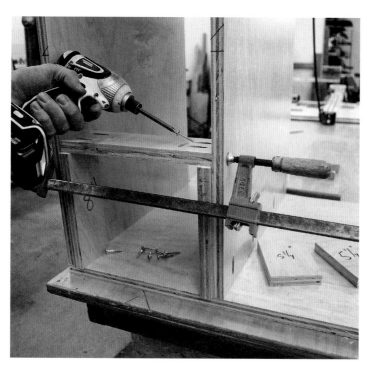

Use two 8-in. strips of plywood to support the horizontal drawer partitions as you screw them to the cabinet partitions.

Installing the Drawer Partitions

Now cut the ¾-in. by 3½-in. by 10½-in. drawer partitions. Pocket-screw with two holes on each end and two holes along the front edge spaced 3 in. from the ends. Place two partitions inside the cabinet flush to the front and back edge and tight against the cabinet end. These will locate the cabinet partitions while screwing. Arrange two more drawer partitions on the top web frame, and hold them in place with clamps. Push one of the vertical partitions in place, and screw the front bottom hole. Work your way along the line of pocket holes, sliding the drawer partition to back up each screw hole. Follow this same procedure to drive the screws in the top of the vertical partition and then repeat for the other interior partition.

Just as I used the drawer partitions to locate the interior cabinet partitions, I'll use some cut scraps to locate the drawer partitions. Cut four pieces of scrap plywood at least 3 in. wide: two at 8 in. long and two at 5½ in. long. Locate the two 8-in. pieces vertically on either side of

Use the 5½-in. plywood scraps to help locate and install the under-sink partition.

where the lower left-hand drawer will go. Slide a drawer partition on top of the scrap 8-in. pieces, flush the front edges, clamp, and screw into place. For the top left drawer, slide the two 5½-in. scraps up until they touch the top of the cabinet and clamp them in place. With the screw holes facing down, slide a drawer partition up until it hits the 5½-in. scrap pieces, clamp, and screw into place. Repeat for the drawer partition on the right-hand side.

Measure the distance between the interior cabinet partitions, and cut a ¾-in. by 3½-in. plywood piece to fit. Use the same 5½-in. scrap pieces to locate the under-sink partition. Next, install the middle drawer partition on the left-hand side of the cabinet. To determine the length of the plywood scrap needed to support the middle partition during installation, set a scrap of ¾-in. plywood on the lower drawer partition and measure the distance to the underside of the upper drawer partition. Divide this number by 2, and cut the two 8-in. scrap pieces to this new dimension. Set the two scrap pieces on top of the lower drawer partition, and locate and install the middle drawer partition in the same manner as before. The cabinet is now ready for the face frame pieces.

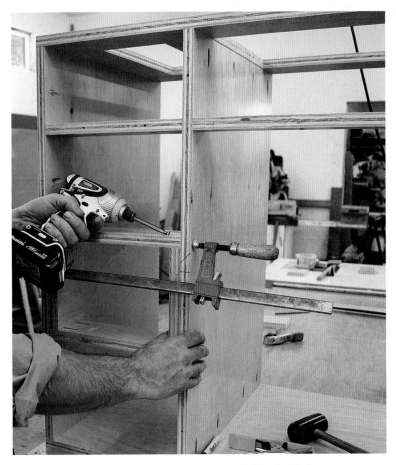

Install the middle drawer partition on the left-hand side last, again using plywood scraps to locate and install the partition.

Attach the end vertical face frame with clamps, then drive pocket screws from the inside.

Clamp the top drawer frame piece to the plywood web frame, and drive a pocket screw into the vertical end frame piece.

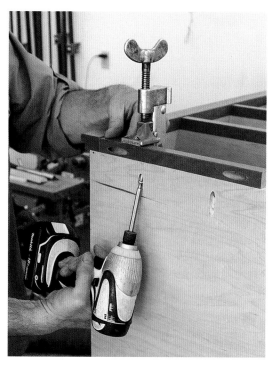

Flip the cabinet onto its back to access the pocket holes on the bottom when installing the last horizontal drawer frame piece.

Installing the Face Frames

Measure the cabinet height (because ¾-in. plywood is slightly less than ¾ in. thick, your cabinet may be just under 30 in. high). Cut the three 1½-in.-wide by 31-in. vertical frame members to this measurement. Starting with the left-side frame piece (which has the ⅜-in. by ⅜-in. rabbet cut from the back side), clamp it into place so that the inside edge is flush with the inside of the cabinet. Use the same tricks to accommodate for the shift as you did for the cabinet parts (see the sidebar on p. 129) and screw the top pocket hole. Move the clamp down and repeat until the piece is fastened.

Measure across the drawer opening to the inside edge of the vertical partition, and check that the measurement is the same at top and bottom. (Since this area will be hidden by drawers, the frames don't have to be perfect: A ¹⁄₃₂-in. variation will not be an issue.) Set a stop block on your saw and cut a scrap to test. Cut the ¾-in. by ¾-in. horizontal drawer frame pieces to the final measurement. These frame pieces will each get two pocket screw holes on one side; ¾ in. is pretty narrow, but if you center the drill on the piece, there should be plenty of wood left on either side of the hole. After drilling the holes, start at the top and clamp a ¾-in. by 10½-in. piece to the top web frame so that it is flush or just below the top of the cabinet (clamping the frame slightly below the top of the cabinet will help minimize shift). You may locate the holes up or down depending on which way is easier for you to drill. Screw the horizontal drawer frame into the vertical end frame. While the clamps are still on, screw the horizontal drawer frame member onto the top web frame. Continue down the cabinet in the same manner, flushing out the top of the drawer frame with the top of the drawer partition. At the bottom, flip the cabinet up on its back, and using a longer clamp, flush the frame piece with the bottom of the cabinet and attach with screws.

Flip the cabinet back down and butt a 1½-in. vertical frame piece against the drawer frame dividers you just installed. Flush the top of the frame piece with the top of the cabinet and

clamp into place. Start with the pocket screw holes that are on the inside of the cabinet partition. You'll notice that there won't be any unwanted creep when screwing in this direction since the screws will pull the vertical frame member tight against the drawer dividers. After the frame piece is attached to the cabinet, screw the drawer dividers onto the frame piece. As you are drilling, place your finger on top of the drawer dividers to feel if there is any shift while screwing. There are plenty of screws in this face frame, so if one shifts more than you'd like, just leave the screw out.

Clamp the third vertical 1½-in. frame piece to the cabinet so that the right edge is flush to the right side of the cabinet partition. Both 1½-in. vertical face-frame pieces will overlap the ¾-in. cabinet partitions toward the sink. You want the face frame to be flush with the cabinet side anywhere there is a drawer so that the drawer slides will not be blocked. Next, compare the measurements across the sink opening at the top of the cabinet, at the under-sink partition,

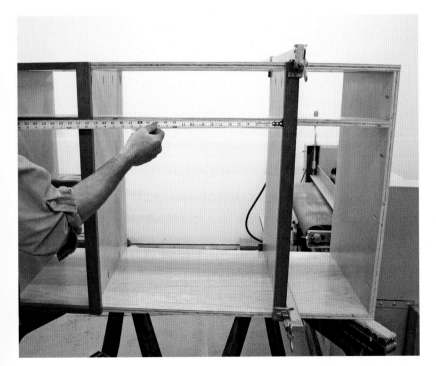

Clamp the third vertical frame piece so that the drawer-side edge is flush with the plywood partition and then measure the sink opening.

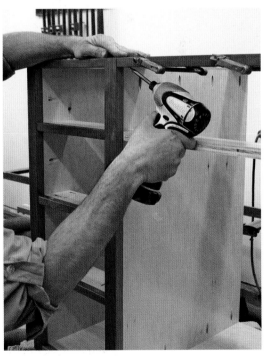

Clamp the top horizontal sink divider to the plywood web, and drive the pocket screws.

To attach the vertical 1½-in. frame to the right of the sink opening, start by screwing the horizontal frame to the vertical frame, then finish by screwing the vertical frame to the cabinet.

and at the bottom of the cabinet to see if there is any difference (see the photo at left on p. 133). A slight difference is to be expected, but if it differs by 1/16 in. or more, cut the horizontal face frames to the exact measurement. If the difference is very slight, cut all three horizontal frames to the same length.

Remove the 1½-in. face frame, and attach the ¾-in. horizontal dividers in the same manner as before. Clamp the third vertical 1½-in. frame in place, and attach by screwing the horizontal frame to the vertical frame first; if you screwed through the cabinet first, it would pull the vertical face frame away from the horizontal dividers. Finish by screwing the vertical frame to the cabinet. Measure across the last opening to the inside edge of the plywood end piece, and repeat the procedure as before, clamping the horizontal divider, screwing it to the vertical face frame, and then screwing it to the cabinet.

Building the Drawers

After the face frame is finished, you're ready to move on to drawer construction. I use the same ¾-in. prefinished maple plywood for the drawer sides as I used for the cabinet, concealing the veneer core of the plywood with ⅛-in. pine edge-banding along the top edge. Pine is easy to mill and matches the tone of the prefinished maple plywood better than hard maple. Covering the veneer core is purely an aesthetic detail. If you're looking to save some time, simply round over and sand the exposed plywood edge.

APPLYING THE EDGE-BANDING

Begin by prepping the edge-banding. Run the pine board from which you'll cut the banding through the planer until the board is just 1/16 in. thicker than the plywood. Then join the edge and rip it to ⅛ in. thick on the tablesaw. Rip the plywood drawer parts to the intended widths (see "Materials" on p. 122). While you are cross-cutting the plywood to length, crosscut the pine at the same time. This means you have to be careful when clamping the edge-banding to make sure the pine completely flushes out with the ends of the drawer stock. A safe approach for beginners would be to cut the edge-band $\frac{1}{16}$ in. longer and trim afterward with a block plane or sanding block.

I like to set up three clamping stations, so that by the time I am done clamping the third drawer side the first one is ready to come out of the clamps. Make sure to set up a caul so that there is even pressure against the edge-banding. I apply glue to the surface with the sawmarks, leaving the joined surface facing up, which minimizes sanding later on. Take your time at the clamps to ensure that the pine completely covers the veneer core of the plywood. After the glue has dried on all the drawer parts, round over the edges with a $\frac{1}{8}$-in. roundover bit on the router table. This should also flush up the $\frac{1}{32}$-in. overhang of the edge-band on the plywood. Use a sander to clean up the machine marks and any remaining overhang of the edge-band.

Apply glue to the edge-band. (Note the three clamping stations.)

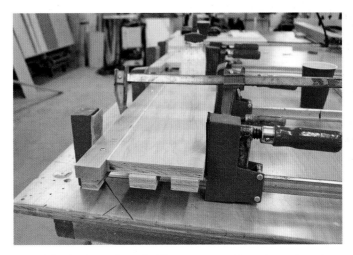

Use a clamping caul to distribute pressure evenly against the edge-banding.

When stacking the freshly glued edge-banded drawer sides, off-set them so that the edge-band is not being pressed down by the drawer side stacked on top of it.

Clean up the edge-band using a $\frac{1}{8}$-in. roundover bit.

The right-angle jig helps you hold the drawer parts as the clamps are tightened. When the parts are positioned, drive the pocket screws.

Slide the drawer bottom into the groove from the back.

Install the drawer clips on the underside of the drawer front.

PREPPING THE DRAWERS

Separate out and label the drawer fronts and backs. I rip ⅛ in. off the width of the drawer fronts so that they butt up against the drawer sides without showing a reveal from the ⅛-in. roundover. The drawer backs get an additional ¾ in. ripped off to allow the drawer bottom to slide in. So for the top drawers with 4⅜-in. drawer sides, the drawer front is 4¼ in. wide and the drawer back is 3½ in. wide. The drawer's sides are all at least ⅞ in. less than the drawer opening in the cabinet.

After ripping the drawer fronts and backs, dado the ¼-in.-wide by 5/16-in.-deep groove for the drawer bottom. This dado is located ½ in. up from the bottom edge of the drawer side and front. The drawer back does not receive a dado because the drawer bottom slides under it. Make sure to test the dado fit on the drawer bottom stock to make sure it's not too tight.

ASSEMBLING THE DRAWERS

After the dadoes are cut, you can pocket-screw the drawer fronts and backs. Two pocket screw holes per butt joint will be plenty. To assemble the drawers, use the same right-angle jig as on the cabinet. Use clamps to hold the drawer fronts in place while screwing. If the drawer front creeps back a hair, don't worry as this will actually create a tighter joint between the drawer sides and the applied cherry drawer front.

Next, measure for and cut the drawer bottoms. Slide the drawer bottoms in and check for square by measuring the diagonal. Pull along the diagonal to bring the drawer square with a clamp. To hold the drawer bottom in place, I use one pocket screw centered into the drawer back. Predrill for this screw so that you don't blow out the plywood.

INSTALLING THE DRAWER SLIDES

To hold the drawer onto the Blum Tandem drawer slides, you'll need to install the drawer clips underneath at the front of the drawer and

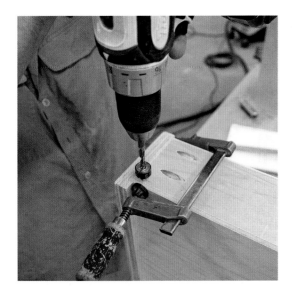

When drilling the ¼-in. index hole in the drawer back, clamp across the drawer bottom and drawer back to keep the plywood core from blowing out.

Drawer Slides

For the drawer slides, I use Blum Tandem plus 562F full-extension drawer runners for cabinets with a depth of 21 in. They can accommodate ¾-in. drawer sides, which work well for pocket screws. With these drawer slides, the drawer width is calculated at ⁷⁄₁₆ in. less than the drawer opening and the drawer length is 18 in. Cutting the drawer sides at 18¹⁄₁₆ in., however, allows the back locating pin on the drawer slide to have a snugger fit and accommodates the slight inward shift when pocket-screwing the drawer backs. The finished drawer side height is ⅞ in. less than the drawer opening.

You can use any number of mechanical drawer slides; just be sure to get the drawer slide spec sheet from the manufacturer before building the drawers.

drill a ¼-in. hole into the drawer back. Start with the clips in the front. There is a left and right clip. Orient each clip so that the orange levers are toward the inside of the drawer. Push the lever into the front corner, and drill with a self-centering bit used for hinges. Drive the #6 by ⅝-in. screw by hand so that it doesn't strip out. Repeat on the opposite side of the drawer.

When the clips are installed on all the drawers, drill the ¼-in. index hole in the drawer backs (see the photo above). The ¼-in. hole is located ⁹⁄₃₂ in. from the edge of the drawer back and ⁷⁄₁₆ in. up from the underside of the drawer bottom. I suggest using a brad-point bit to keep the hole clean. Drill the holes ⅜ in. deep.

The drawer slides sit on top of the drawer partitions and are set back 1 in. from the ¾-in. horizontal face frame. This gives the finished drawer front just a slight setback from the face frame. To support the drawer slide during installation, I measure and cut a 3-in.-wide strip of plywood so that it is the same height off the cabinet bottom as the top edge of the drawer divider. To mark the cut, simply slide the support into the cabinet and pull it up against the drawer

dividers and make a mark. You'll need to make one of these for each drawer opening. To help the support stand up, pocket-screw two of them together.

Start at the top and work your way down (otherwise the drawer slide will get in the way of the drawer slide support). The drawer slides, like the drawer clips, come in right- and left-hand sides. The back of the drawer slide has the locating pin. The screw holes on the drawer slide go against the cabinet side. Place the slide support at the back of the cabinet and against the cabinet side. Set the drawer slide on top of the drawer partition and support (see the top left photo on p. 138). Use a try square to set the slide 1 in. back from the front of the ¾-in. face frame. Holding the drawer slide in place with your hand, drill a hole using the self-centering bit. Set the drawer slide with a #6 screw, and check to make sure it didn't shift during drilling. If it moved from the

The drawer-slide support keeps the back of the drawer slide at the same height as the drawer partition, which ensures that the slide is installed parallel to the cabinet bottom.

Use a try square to set the drawer slide 1 in. back from the front of the horizontal face frame.

Check the drawer front setback using a scrap of ¾-in. stock.

After setting the first pair of drawer slides, check the reveal between the drawer front and the face frame. Pull out the drawer slides, and set the drawer on top of the runners. Push the drawer in until you hear the click of the clips on both sides. Use a scrap piece of ¾-in. stock to check the drawer slide setback with the face frame. To remove the drawer, pull it out and squeeze the clips, then pull up and out.

FITTING THE DRAWER FRONTS

With the drawers constructed and slides installed, you can cut the drawer fronts to fit inside the face-frame opening. Mill your drawer stock at ¾ in. thick. I shoot for a ¹⁄₁₆-in. gap on all four sides of a finish-sanded drawer front. When rough-fitting the fronts to the opening, I use a ¹⁄₁₆-in. shim at the bottom and on one side. Check that the reveals on the opposite side are parallel to the opening. At this point, the gap on the top and opposite side of the shims should be around ¹⁄₃₂ in. Sanding the machine marks off of the drawer front edge will remove the remaining ¹⁄₃₂ in. of wood to achieve the ¹⁄₁₆-in. gap on all four sides.

1-in. setback, remove the screw and drill again. There are plenty of holes in the drawer slide for installation. A slight shift won't be a problem, but always check to make sure it didn't move ¹⁄₁₆ in. or more. There are three spots for installing screws on these drawer slides. Two screws in each hole cluster is plenty.

DOORS AND DRAWER FRONTS

5⅛ in.

5⅛ in. ← 21⅜ in. →

← 10⅜ in. →

6⅜ in.

6⅜ in.

18⅜ in.

18⅜ in.

18⅜ in.

21⅜ in.

7⅞ in.
← 10⅜ in. →

← 7⅛ in. →

← 7⅛ in. →

← 6⅜ in. →

2¼ in.

2¼ in.

2¼ in.

← 6⅝ in. →

← 6⅝ in. →

← 5⅞ in. →

Before sanding and finishing the drawer fronts, make final installation easier by drilling out for the press-in drawer front locaters. These are small plastic plugs that have a floating washer in them. Purchase the plugs, drill bit, and hole locaters all at the same time. To install, drill two 20 mm holes in the back of the drawer front, located toward the ends so as not to interfere with the handles. Drill the holes about ⁷⁄₁₆ in. deep so that the plastic plugs will seat flush with the drawer back. Place two hole locaters into the 20 mm holes and, with the ¹⁄₁₆-in. shims

Use a ¹⁄₁₆-in. shim under each corner to help fit the drawer front to the opening. (You'll need to first install a temporary plywood face frame on the right-hand side of the cabinet to help fit the drawer front in the top right drawer.)

in place, press the drawer front against the drawer box to locate the holes for the drawer. Use a 3/16-in. bit to drill out the hole. The drawer front locaters will need #8-32 by 1⅛-in. screws. After the holes are located in the drawer box, you can pound the drawer front locaters into the drawer fronts with a mallet. Hammer them until they are flush with the surface. The drawer fronts are now ready for finish-sanding and oil coats.

Drawer front locaters: The round white plastic plug, which fits into a hole drilled in the back of the drawer front, makes installing flush-front face-frame drawer fronts a simple process.

The metal dowels have a pointed center that helps transfer the location of the screw hole to the drawer box.

Use a 3/16-in. bit to drill out the hole at the small indentation left by the metal point.

Building the End Panel

The end panel shares many milling steps with the doors, but it's easier to tackle them separately. The front post adjacent to the end panel is made from two pieces: a ⅞-in. by 1⅝-in. by 30-in. and a ⅞-in. by 3-in. by 30-in. cherry strip glued together with a 45-degree bevel to make the two pieces look like a thick corner post. The back post is ⅞ in. thick by 3 in. wide and has a scribe dado on the inside of the back edge to facilitate installation. The top and bottom rails are 3 in. wide and ¾ in. thick (⅛ in. narrower than the posts to echo the ⅛-in. surface step detail used on the front face frame). The panel is ¼-in. cherry plywood.

CUTTING THE END POST

To keep the grain of the front post's 1⅝-in. face and 3-in. face complementary, rough out the stock for both pieces from a 5¼-in.-wide board. Plane and join the material to dimension, leaving the front post stock uncut at 5¼ in. wide. Cut the front and back post to the cabinet height. Rip the wide front post to 1⅞ in. wide. If there was any bowing after ripping, join the outside edge on both the 1⅞-in. and 3¼-in. pieces again. Set the tablesaw blade at 45 degrees. Use a try square to mark the bevel, allowing a +1/16-in. margin of error, as gluing up a 45-degree

Mark the miter location so that the inside face is the width of the panel plus ¹⁄₁₆ in.

Check that the front miter touches the horizontal face frame and overhangs the plywood end panel.

With the saw turned off, check the miter and saw fence settings.

WORK SMART

If mitering the corner post sounds too complicated, you can simply pocket-screw two boards together to create the corner post.

bevel edge sometimes causes a small amount of shift.

Set the saw fence to cut the line. To check the fence setting, just barely start the cut, then pull it back and look at the sawmark to make sure it is located correctly with the pencil line. Set the post on the cabinet to triple-check that the cut won't come up short. Rip the 45-degree bevel. Take the 3¼-in. piece and set the saw fence so that the long measurement on the bevel is 3 in. This cut is less critical than the other cut and just needs to be 3 in. wide.

ROUTING THE PANEL GROOVE

Before gluing up the corner post, you need to rout for the ¼-in. panel groove. This will be a stop cut, meaning the groove will start and stop about 2⅝ in. from the ends. Stop cuts are easiest using a slot cutter on a router, but they can be done with a ¼-in. straight bit, too. Using a ³⁄₁₆-in. slot cutter and making two passes allows for fine-tuning the fit of the plywood in the slot (a standard ¼-in. bit may be a bit sloppy). Set the slot cutter ¼ in. above the tabletop and ⁵⁄₁₆ in. deep. On the router fence, use tape to label "start" and "end" where the bit will start and

Rout for the panel groove in the end-panel frame members.

Four biscuits down the length of the corner posts help keep it aligned during glue-up.

stop its cut (see the top photo at left). On the faces of the side posts, label where the groove will start and stop. (The top and bottom rails will not need this labeling because they have through cuts.) It is always helpful to use a scrap piece of wood to test the cuts to avoid ruining the good pieces.

When the router bit is set correctly, make the first pass on the top and bottom rails. To start the stop cuts on the post, angle the stock in so that the start mark on the cherry face lines up with the start mark on the fence, push through the cut until the end mark on the face meets the end mark on the fence, and angle the stock away from the fence. Once you've made the first passes, raise the $\frac{3}{16}$-in. slot cutter, cut just the first 2 in. of the scrap piece of wood, and test the fit on the edge of the panel material. If the fit is acceptable, repeat the process on the end-post material. The front and back grooves will need to be chiseled out a bit to fit the panel since the arc of the slot cutter is curved at the ends. Use the top or bottom rail, and position it on top of a side post to mark the end of the slot. Chisel to the mark.

GLUING UP THE FRONT CORNER POST

Now the front corner post can be glued up. Mark and biscuit the mating pieces for the front post; four biscuits will be plenty to align and strengthen the joint. Place the 3-in.-wide post on the edge of the bench, then glue the biscuit slots and pound in biscuits. Take the mating front piece and apply glue to the surface. Press the two pieces together, and use a mallet to make sure the ends match perfectly. Apply clamps, alternating between faces and double-checking that the ends still match up. Check that the outside corner is square during clamp-up and, if necessary, move the clamps to either side to pull it into square. After the glue has dried on the front post, remove the clamps and check the fit on the cabinet.

Lay out for the end-panel assembly, checking that the rail length measures 20¼ in. between the inside of the front post and the back edge of the back post.

CUTTING TO WIDTH

Assuming that the front post fits, measure the side of the plywood cabinet and add ½ in. to this dimension to account for the ¼-in. melamine cabinet back and ¼-in. scribe rabbet. The measurement should be around 20¼ in. Set the end panel posts face down on a bench. Space them apart so that the measurement from the inside edge of the corner post to the outside edge of the back post is 20¼ in. (see the photo above). Then measure the distance between the inside faces to get the length of the side panel rails. Cut a scrap piece, check the measurement, and cut the finished rails to this measurement.

Drill the pocket screw holes on the back side of the rails. Dry-assemble the posts and rails, and measure for the plywood panel. Subtract ⅛ in. from the panel groove dimension on both height and width. Cut the ¼-in. cherry panel and check the fit. Before applying a coat of oil, cut a ⅝-in.-wide by ¼-in.-deep dado into the back side of the back post to help scribe onto the wall during installation. Finish-sand the pieces and apply oil if prefinishing.

Milling the Door Stock

Mill the door stock so that the stiles are just over ¼ in. thick and the rails just over ⅝ in. thick. As a design detail, the double doors underneath the sink have two different widths of stiles: The out-side stiles are 2¼ in. wide and the inside stiles are 1¾ in. wide. The stiles on the garbage pull-out are both 2¼ in. wide. The rails on all the doors are 2¼ in. wide. Measure the door height opening; if the measurement varies slightly from side to side, take the greatest and subtract 1/16 in. Cut the door stiles to this length.

While milling the groove for the door panel, you can leave the door rails long. Set the slot cutter so that it is 3/16 in. above the benchtop. Repeat the stop-cut labeling process from the end panel with the door stiles. Use scrapwood to check the fit of the groove on the cherry MDF door panel stock. When the grooves have been cut, chisel out the stop cut on the stiles.

Measure the width of the door opening. A finished sanded door has a maximum gap of 1/16 in. on all four sides. Allow for a 1/16-in. gap for assembly, and plan on removing another 1/16 in. to fit the door in the opening. Measure across the garbage pullout opening, and subtract 1/16 in. Subtract the combined width of the door stiles to calculate the rails for the pullout door. Next, measure for the doors under the sink at the top and bottom of the opening. Take the larger number and subtract ⅛ in. Subtract the combined width of the four stiles from this measurement. Divide this number in half to get the length of the rails. Cut four small scraps to this measurement, and align the door stiles flat on the bench to see if this measurement will work

Dry-fit the doors to make sure the panel fits correctly.

(it must be no more than ⅛ in. less than the door opening under the sink). When the length of the rails has been determined, cut the stock.

DRY-FIT THE DOORS

Dry-fit the door stock, and measure for the door panel heights. The width of the door panels will be ½ in. more than the length of the rails. Cut the panels and dry-fit. If the dry fit is acceptable, drill two pocket screw holes on each end of the back side of the rails, making sure to avoid drilling too close to the panel groove. Finish-sand the front and inside faces of the door frame and both sides of the door panel. Prefinish both sides of the panel and the front and inside faces of the door frame stock.

While waiting for the end panels and door finish to dry, cut and install the ¼-in. melamine back. Measure the diagonals on the cut back panel. If the back panel is square, use it to square up the cabinet by pinning the bottom first, then flushing up a corner and holding it in place with a clamp. Nail off the perimeter and partitions.

Assembling the End Panel

To assemble the end panel, start by clamping the back rail to the right-angle jig. Slide the panel into the groove, and place a rail in position to be attached. There is a ⅛-in. step down from the vertical post to the horizontal rail. When clamping with the face clamp, you'll need a ⅛-in. shim to make the thickness of the rail the same as the post. A leather pad on the face clamp will help keep it from marring the finished surface. Flush up the edge of the rail with the end of the post, and clamp with the face clamps. Carefully drive two screws through the rail into the post.

Move the right-angle jig to the other side and repeat with the next rail. Align the front post onto the assembly, flush up an end, and clamp. Drive pocket screws and repeat on the last corner, making sure to flush up the ends exactly and drive the screws with a moderate to slow drill speed. Set the end panel into place and

Use the face clamp to hold the corner post tight when driving the pocket screws through the rail.

Starting with the screws through the horizontal drawer frame pieces, attach the end panel to the cabinet.

Assemble the door in the usual way, using the right-angle jig and face clamp.

Apply glue to the pocket screw holes and tap in the plugs. Allow to dry before sanding flush.

A final sanding of the plugs brings them flush to the surface.

hold with a clamp. Screw through the horizontal face frame first, then screw from the end plywood panel into the front post and finish with three screws through the back of the cabinet plywood into the back 3-in. post on the end panel.

Assembling the Doors

The process for assembling the doors is the same as for the end panel, using the right-angle jig and ⅛-in. clamp shim with the face clamp. Start by clamping a stile to the right-angle jig, slide the door panel into place, and locate the bottom rail. Clamp with the face clamp and the ⅛-in. shim and carefully screw. A slow drill speed is preferred. Locate the opposite rail and clamp with the face clamp and shim, making sure the edge of the rail is flush with the end of the stile. Screw the rail into place. Locate the opposite stile, flush up the end with the rail edge, clamp, and screw into place. Finish by clamping and screwing the last corner of the door.

Pocket Hole Plugs

As I imagine I've made clear by this point, I prefer designs that work without having to use pocket hole plugs. But there are situations where you need plugs (as on the vanity doors here) and they are very handy to have. There are several species of plugs available from Kreg and even different-colored plastic pegs that press in without the need to flush-sand.

Router Plug Cleanup

It's surprising how much work it takes to sand or rout the plugs down. There is quite a bit of wood to remove and eight plug holes per door. I used a router with a scrap of ¾-in. plywood to raise the router above the plugs. Set the router bit so that it cuts just above the surface of the door. Be careful, as it's easy to gouge the door with the router bit.

A belt sander also makes quick work of flushing out the plugs but has the same potential to gouge the back of the door. A random-orbit sander will also do the job. It will be much slower at removing the wood but less susceptible to damaging the door.

Check the fit of the doors in the opening.

With the doors assembled, plug the pocket holes with cherry plugs. Use a generous amount of glue, as the plugs have a loose fit in the hole. Tap the plugs into place with a mallet. Next, belt-sand or rout the plugs flush to the surface of the door (see the sidebar above).

FITTING THE DOORS

Check the fit of the doors in the cabinet openings. When the doors are finish-sanded, there should be a gap of around ¹⁄₁₆ in. on all four sides. But when fitting the doors with the table-saw and jointer, make the gap a bit smaller, anticipating that a bit more wood will be removed when finish-sanding. To do this, use a ¹⁄₁₆-in. shim at the bottom and on one side of the door, but leave less than ¹⁄₁₆ in. of a gap at the top and opposite side. With double doors, there will be a ¹⁄₁₆-in. gap on either side of the opening and ¹⁄₁₆ in. between the doors in the middle. When rough-fitting double doors to the opening, allow for a ¹⁄₁₆-in. gap on the outside but have the doors touching in the middle. By the time all four edges of the doors have been finish-sanded, there will be a 1/16-in. gap in the middle.

INSTALLING THE HINGES

Before finish-sanding, drill out the door backs for the hinges. I use Blum concealed Euro hinges, but there are many varieties. Euro hinges require you to drill a hole in the back of the door for the hinge cup to fit into. A matching 35 mm drill bit is required to drill the holes. The hinge is held in place with five #6 by 5/8-in. screws. Euro hinges allow for adjustments both vertically and horizontally, which allows you to fine-tune the door fit after the cabinet is installed.

Drill the holes in the door 4 in. down from the top and bottom. The edge of the 35 mm hole should be about 1/4 in. from the edge of the door. The depth of the hole should be just over 1/2 in. so that the hinge perimeter sits flush on the surface of the door. Align both hinges in the door and, with a straightedge against the flat side of the hinge cups, predrill with a self-centering bit for the #6 screws. Attach the hinge cups to the doors.

Install the hinge bases in the cabinet next. First, attach a strip of 3/4-in. plywood to the inside of the cabinet so that the side where the hinge bases will be installed is flush with the 1 1/2-in. vertical face frame edge. I used a 3-in.-wide scrap and drilled from the drawer box side with four pocket screws. The bases will be set 4 1/16 in. on-center from the top and bottom edge of the door opening. There are three holes per base.

Building a jig to align the holes is easy enough (and will be useful the next time you use Euro hinges), but measuring and drilling the holes one at a time is simple, too. The front two holes are located 2 7/16 in. from the front edge of the vertical face frame post and are 1 1/4 in. apart. Don't worry about drilling the third hole until the bases are installed in the cabinet.

The Euro hinge arm attaches to the hinge base with a clip. There is a small metal bar at the cup side of the hinge arm that locates in a small groove in the front of the hinge base. A small

Use a straightedge against the Euro hinges to help align them when drilling the screw holes.

A strip of plywood is needed to bring the hinges out far enough to reach around the face frame. Attach the hinge bases to the strip with screws.

clip on the end of the hinge arm fastens to the end of the hinge base. Locate the bar on the arm first, and then press the end of the arm onto the base until it clicks (see the top right photo on p. 148). To remove, squeeze the clip on the end of the hinge arm and pull out. If it isn't clipping, loosen the one screw on the hinge base that allows the up-and-down adjustment and try again.

When all the hinge arms and bases have been installed on the doors and cabinets, attach the doors. There are three screws for adjustment, two on the hinge arm and one on the base. The front screw moves the door side to side relative to the $\frac{1}{16}$-in. gap, while the back screw on the arm moves the door in and out relative to the face frame. The one screw on the base moves the door up and down relative to the $\frac{1}{16}$-in. gap on the door opening. You'll need to install a door stop on the underside of the sink tip-out partition; clamp one temporarily while fitting the doors. Adjust the doors so that there is a consistent reveal on all four sides; if the fit is good, the door edges and backs are ready to be finish-sanded and oiled.

The hinges clip onto the bases, which makes installation a snap.

Installing the Drawer Fronts

Once the drawer fronts have been given their final finish coat, they can be installed on the drawers with two #8-32 by $1\frac{1}{8}$-in. screws. Use a strip of blue tape over the top edge of the drawer front to serve as a temporary handle. Push the drawer front side to side and up and down until the reveal is equal on all four sides. Then predrill

Thread the #8-32 screws into the plastic plug locaters in the drawer front (left), then add two pocket screws to secure the drawer front in its final location (above).

and screw two 1¼-in. pocket screws (while the adjusters help locate the drawer front, pocket screws make sure it stays put).

INSTALLING THE TIP-OUT TRAY

Under the sink is a tip-out tray, and as with the doors under the sink, you'll need to install a small 3-in. scrap of plywood on the cabinet sides so that the tip-out hinges won't hit the 1½-in. vertical face frame. I used a ½-in. shim to raise the tip-out hinge during predrilling. The 1½-in. face frame is just proud of the ¾-in. plywood spacer. Slide the tip-out hinge until it touches the back side of the face frame, and screw the top hole. Repeat on the opposite side. Use a ¾-in. scrap of cherry to represent the tip-out drawer front, and press it against the tip-out hinge. When the reveal of the cherry scrap is parallel to the front face frame, drive another screw into the tip-out hinge. Repeat on the opposite side.

Locate the tip-out drawer front with ¹⁄₁₆-in. shims, and mark the screw hole slots. The slots are elongated so that minor adjustments can be made. The reality with these tip-out accessories is that it is trial and error until the fit is acceptable. Luckily, it is hard to spot, so multiple screw holes will not be noticed.

INSTALLING THE PULL-OUT GARBAGE CONTAINER

The lower right-hand compartment of the cabinet will house a pull-out garbage container. This was a bit difficult to locate and, to be honest, needed a bit of aftermarket adjustments with a file to make work. It is a nice accessory, but there are a wider variety of options on deeper cabinets. For 21-in.-deep vanities, the pickings are slim. I followed the directions on assembly and mounted it in the cabinet. There are several slotted screw holes that allow you to move the pull-out slides in both directions to fine-tune the fit. Attaching the door to the door mounts is made a bit easier by using the double-stick tape

Install the hinges for the tip-out tray on both sides of the under-sink opening.

When installing the hardware for the pull-out garbage container, use a scrap of plywood to make sure that the runners are mounted parallel.

included with the hardware, but as with the tip-out hinges, it is a case of trial and error. Waiting until the cabinet is installed before installing the door is preferable, as slight variations to the cabinets sometimes occur.

Installing the Base

The cabinet base is made of ¾-in. by 4-in. strips of plywood that are pocket-screwed together. A ¼-in. by 4-in. strip of cherry plywood serves as the finish face to the toe kick. The cabinet depth is 21 in., and I built the toe kick 17 in. deep. Planning on a ¼-in. shim in the back and the ¼-in. finished cherry face in front puts the toe kick setback at around 3½ in. from the front of the cabinet. The toe kick base is 47 in. long, the same as the cabinet box without the end panel. Adding the ¼-in. cherry face to the end still leaves a ½-in. overhang on the side of the cabi-

net. Having the toe-kick width the same as the cabinet body without the end panel ensures that the cabinet partitions will all be supported directly through to the floor.

The four toe-kick stretchers line up exactly underneath the cabinet partitions. I attach four additional strips flat side up to these short stretchers to assist in screwing the cabinet to the toe kick. Rip and crosscut the two 47-in. stretchers and eight 15½-in. short stretchers. Pocket-screw two holes on either end on all of the 15½-in. stretchers. On the four short stretchers that will be flat side up, pocket-screw an additional two holes on the sides.

If the toe kick will be sitting on a wood floor, pocket screw holes on the front and back stretchers can help secure it to the floor; drill these now but take into account that the short stretchers may get in the way of some of the holes on the back stretchers. Assemble the pairs

Clamp the base upright to the bench to make it easier to reach all the pocket holes.

If necessary, use a combination of shims and wood scraps to level the base.

of short stretchers and then, starting at one end, attach the stretchers to the 47-in. front strip. Finish by attaching the back stretcher to the toe-kick assembly.

Installing the Cabinet

To begin the cabinet installation, use shims to level the base (see the photo above). The toe kick should be about ¾ in. from the wall on the short side with a ¼-in. gap on the back; this allows for the 1½-in. vertical face frame and ensures that the toe kick lines up under the cabinet. When the toe kick is level, use the pocket holes in the front and rear stretcher to attach it to the floor. If the floor is not wood, screw through both the back and side of the toe kick into the wall studs.

Set the cabinet on the base and slide it into place. Check again to see that it is level. You may need to insert shims between the cabinet and toe kick to level the cabinet again. Check to see that the end panel and front face frame sit nicely against the wall with an even gap. If the walls are

A couple of screws along the top edge into the wall studs help secure the vanity.

Attach the Euro hinges to the doors using a Phillips screwdriver to adjust the hinges for a perfect fit.

Finish up by installing the knob handles on the doors and drawer faces.

out of plumb, you'll need to scribe the cabinet to the walls. Check the cabinet fit and then screw the cabinet to the base. Add additional screws through the top web frame into the wall studs, making sure not to pull the cabinet out of square. Use a shim to maintain the distance between the wall and cabinet.

INSTALLING THE DRAWERS AND DOORS

Now you can install the drawers and the doors under the sink. Use a Phillips screwdriver to adjust the door hinges for a perfect fit. Install the door on the pull-out garbage compartment using the double-stick tape included with the slides and 1/16-in. shims. Be prepared to do this process a couple of times, as it rarely turns out right the first time. There are plenty of holes in the door-mounting hardware to give you a second and third chance at installing it correctly. Be patient.

The final job is to install the handles. On the pull-out garbage door, it's best to center the handle on the top rail of the door rather than locating it on the stile (as is done with the under-sink drawers). On the drawers, you might need extra-long screws to reach through the drawer front and drawer box; there are usually screws of several lengths in each package of knobs or handles. Commercial or shop-made handle jigs can be a big help when marking for the handles because they keep you from making measurement mistakes. If you're not using a jig, measure the hole location from one side of the drawer fronts and keep it consistent all the way down the bank of drawers.

Once all the handles are installed, all that remains is to install a countertop for your vanity . . . but that's another book!

DRESSER

There are 171 pocket screws in this Craftsman dresser, but to find one you'd have to be down on your knees with your head against the floor looking under it. In addition to the case and drawers, the breadboard top and even the drawer handles use pocket screws for assembly, but none of them are visible to the casual observer. This dresser is a big project with lots of parts, but pocket hole joinery puts it within reach of beginning woodworkers and using biscuits to help the parts being pocket-screwed streamlines the assembly process.

The meat of the case is in the post and panel sides. A ¾-in. veneer plywood makes up the panel, which is attached to the posts and rails via biscuits and pocket screws. Building the post and panel sides is the most challenging part of the project since the width of the panels and length of the rails must be exactly the same. While this seems like a simple enough challenge, the fact that you rip the width of the panel on the tablesaw but crosscut the rails on a chopsaw or sliding table means two different machines and settings for one measurement. Add to this the fact that trimming small amounts of wood

(Continued on p. 158)

MATERIALS

QUANTITY	PART	ACTUAL SIZE	CONSTRUCTION NOTES
DRESSER CASE			
4	Posts	1¾ in. × 2 in. × 41 in.	White oak
2	Top side rails	1⁹⁄₁₆ in. × 2 in. × 14 in.+ (cut exact length later)	White oak
2	Bottom side rails	1⁹⁄₁₆ in. × 2½ in. × 14 in.+ (cut exact length later)	White oak
1	Bottom front rail	¾ in. × 2½ in. × 32 in.	White oak
1	Bottom	¾ in. × 17 in.+ × 32 in. (cut exact depth later)	Plywood
2	Side panels	¾ in. × 14 in.+ × 32½ in. (cut exact width of panel later)	Plywood
1	Back panel	¼ in. × 33 in. × 35½ in.	Plywood
4	Front horizontal drawer dividers	¾ in. × 1¾ in. × 32 in.	White oak
1	Back top frame	¾ in. × 2½ in. × 32 in.	Alder
1	Back bottom frame	¾ in. × 1½ in. × 32 in.	Alder
1	Top frame short connector	¾ in. × 2½ in. × 13 in.+ (cut exact length later)	Alder
1	Top drawer partition	¾ in. × 5¾ in. × 15½ in.+ (cut exact length later)	Plywood
1	Top drawer partition edge-band solid wood	¾ in. × 1¾ in. × 5¾ in.	White oak
2	Biscuit spacers and drawer-slide nailers	⅝ in. × 2 in. × 32½ in.	Alder
DRAWER FRONTS			
2	Top drawers	¾ in. × 5¾ in. × 15⅝ in. (cut exact length during fitting for all drawer fronts)	White oak
1	Second drawer	¾ in. × 7 in. × 32 in.	White oak
1	Third drawer	¾ in. × 8½ in. × 32 in.	White oak
1	Bottom drawer	¾ in. × 10¼ in. × 32 in.	White oak

QUANTITY	PART	ACTUAL SIZE	CONSTRUCTION NOTES
DRAWER BOXES			
4	Top sides	¾ in. × 4¾ in. × 15¹⁄₁₆ in.	Alder
2	Top fronts	¾ in. × 4⁹⁄₁₆ in. × 13¹¹⁄₁₆ in.	Alder
2	Top backs	¾ in. × 3¹³⁄₁₆ in. × 13¹¹⁄₁₆ in.	Alder
2	Second sides	¾ in. × 6 in. × 15¹⁄₁₆ in.	Alder
1	Second front	¾ in. × 5¹³⁄₁₆ in. × 30¹⁄₁₆ in.	Alder
1	Second back	¾ in. × 5¹⁄₁₆ in. × 30¹⁄₁₆ in.	Alder
2	Third sides	¾ in. × 7½ in. × 15¹⁄₁₆ in.	Alder
1	Third front	¾ in. × ⁵⁄₁₆ in. × 30¹⁄₁₆ in.	Alder
1	Third back	¾ in. × 6⁹⁄₁₆ in. × 30¹⁄₁₆ in.	Alder
2	Bottom sides	¾ in. × 9¼ in. × 15¹⁄₁₆ in.	Alder
1	Bottom front	¾ in. × 9¹⁄₁₆ in. × 30¹⁄₁₆ in.	Alder
1	Bottom back	¾ in. × 8⁵⁄₁₆ in. × 30¹⁄₁₆ in.	Alder
3	Bottom panels	14⁹⁄₁₆ in. deep × 30⅝ in. wide	¼-in. maple plywood
2	Bottom panels	14⁹⁄₁₆ in. deep × 14¼ in. wide	¼-in. maple plywood
5	Drawer slides	563F3810B 15 in. Tandem Blumotion ¾ in.	
5	Drawer clip sets	T51.1801 L LH Tandem Lock Device 563/569	
BREADBOARD TOP			
2	Ends	¾ in. × 3 in. × 19¾ in.	White oak
1	Center panel	¾ in. × 19⅜ in. × 32 in.	White oak
HANDLES (FINISHED DIMENSIONS; ROUGH-MILL HANDLES 17 IN. LONG)			
10	End blocks	⅞ in. × 1⅛ in. × 1⅛ in.	White oak
3	Large handles	¾ in. × 1¼ in. × 16 in.	White oak
2	Small handles	¾ in. × 1¼ in. × 8 in.	White oak

Front view

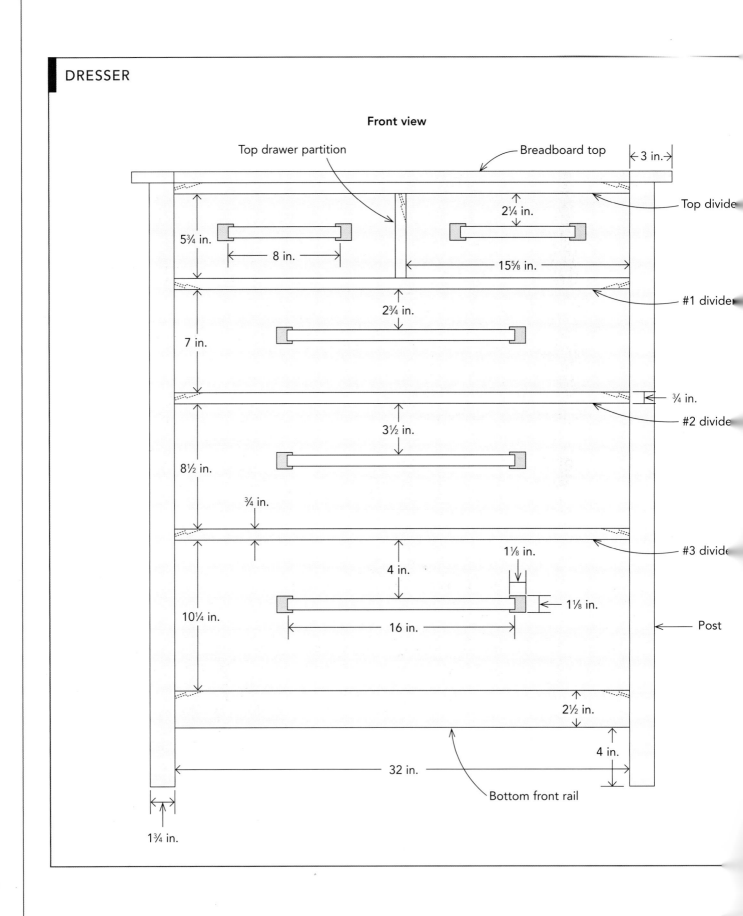

Top drawer partition

Breadboard top

3 in.

Top divider

2¼ in.

5¾ in.

8 in.

15⅝ in.

#1 divider

2¾ in.

7 in.

¾ in.

#2 divider

3½ in.

8½ in.

¾ in.

#3 divider

1⅛ in.

4 in.

1⅛ in.

10¼ in.

16 in.

Post

2½ in.

32 in.

4 in.

Bottom front rail

1¾ in.

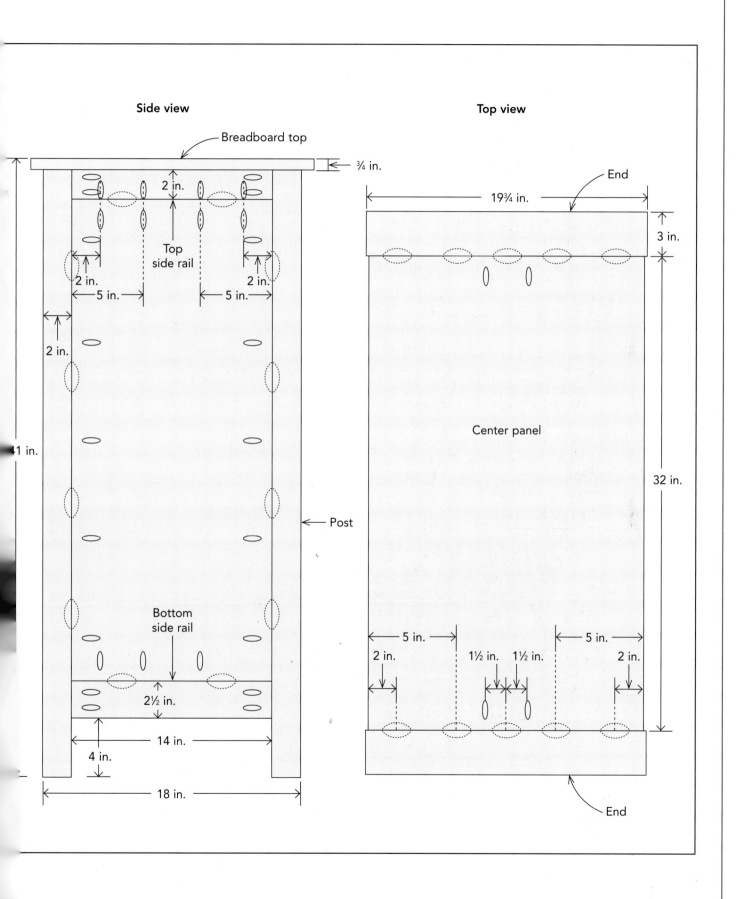

Side view

Breadboard top

¾ in.

2 in.

Top side rail

2 in.

5 in.

2 in.

5 in.

2 in.

1 in.

Post

2½ in.

Bottom side rail

14 in.

4 in.

18 in.

Top view

End

19¾ in.

3 in.

Center panel

32 in.

5 in.

5 in.

2 in.

1½ in. 1½ in.

2 in.

End

from a 1½-in.-wide piece of white oak without blade deflection or accidentally taking too much off means it's best to hit the bull's-eye on the first try.

Dresser Case: Stock Preparation

Start by cutting and milling the material to size, but leave the rails long and the plywood panels at least 1 in. wide to begin with. Mill the drawer fronts to thickness, but don't rip or crosscut them to length yet. The depth of the bottom panel should be left ½ in. long until the exact location of the groove for the back panel is determined. The bottom panel, lower front rail, and all of the drawer partitions are the same length and should be cut to length at the same time.

To dial in the side rails and panels, start by setting a cutoff block at 14 in. and cut all four rails. Set the tablesaw fence at 14 in. and rip a scrap of plywood. Compare the width of the scrap plywood with the length of the rails. Continue to dial in the rip fence setting with scraps of plywood until the tablesaw is ripping panels exactly the same width as the rails. To check your results, press the posts against the side panels and rails and look for any gaps. A slightly proud panel can be flushed up after assembly with a block plane, but a proud rail will be more difficult to adjust squarely.

Cutting the Biscuits

When you've cut the rails and panels to length, lay out all the parts in order. Use biscuits and pocket screws set on top of the panel to help establish their location: There are four biscuits on the sides between the panel and posts and two biscuits on the top and bottom between the panel and rails. The rails and posts have a ³⁄₁₆-in. step at the butt joint on the outside but are flush on the inside face. The panels are stepped back ³⁄₁₆ in. from the face of the rails and ⅜ in. from the face of the posts. On the inside, the panel is stepped back ⅝ in. from both the posts and rails. Mill two strips of alder ⅝ in. by 2 in. by 32½ in. These strips will be used under the biscuit jointer when cutting the biscuit slots in the post and rails to establish the ⅝-in.

Setting biscuits and pocket screws on top of the dresser parts helps to determine their location.

SIDE PANEL DETAIL

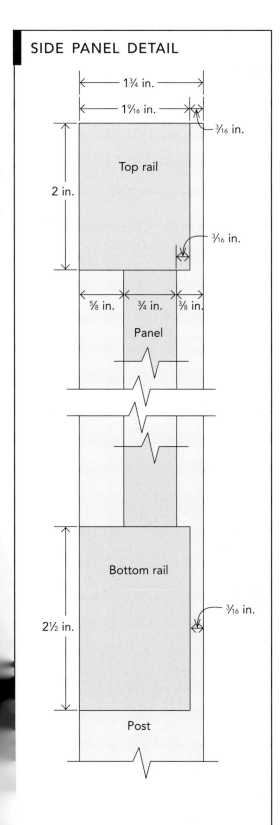

Top rail

1¾ in.
1⁹⁄₁₆ in.
³⁄₁₆ in.
³⁄₁₆ in.

2 in.

⅝ in.   ¾ in.   ⅜ in.

Panel

Bottom rail

2½ in.

³⁄₁₆ in.

Post

With the front of the panel facing up, use the benchtop as a fence reference for the biscuit jointer.

A pair of ⅝-in. alder strips elevates the biscuit jointer to the proper height to cut the posts and rails. These alder strips will be used later inside the dresser to help attach the drawer slides.

step between them and the panel. Later, the alder strips will be installed in the back of the dresser to give the drawer slides something to screw to.

The biscuit slots on the sides of the panels are located at approximately 4½ in. and 12 in. measuring from both the top and bottom on each side (or measuring from the top, 4½ in., 12 in., 20½ in., 28 in.). The biscuit slots on the top and bottom edge of the panel are located at 3½ in.

from each corner. On the corner posts, the biscuit slots are located 6½ in. and 14 in. from the top and 11 in. and 18½ in. from the bottom (or measuring from the top, 6½ in., 14 in., 22½ in., and 30 in.). The biscuit slots in the top and bottom rails are located 3½ in. from each end. Using the benchtop as a reference face and with the good side of the panels facing up, cut the biscuit slots on all four sides of both panels (see the top photo on p. 159). To biscuit the posts, set the 2-in. outer face of the posts up and the ⅝-in. alder

strips under the biscuit jointer to cut the slots. To biscuit the rails, set the outside faces up, position the ⅝-in. alder strips under the biscuit jointer, and cut the slots in the top and bottom rails.

Drilling the Pocket Holes

When combining pocket screws with biscuits, I try to place them as close to each other as possible so that the biscuit will do a good job of keeping the pocket screw from shifting the joint. Measured locations for the five pocket holes from the top corner of the panel are 2½ in., 10 in., 16 in., 22 in., and 29½ in. on each side. The location of the four pocket holes for the top and bottom edges are 2 in., 5 in., 9 in., and 12 in. from either end. The top and bottom rails get two pocket holes on each end;

Drill pocket holes in the panels to attach the rail and posts.

Lay out the location of the pocket holes next to the biscuits. Make the mark high enough so that it can be seen over the pocket hole jig.

Drill two pocket holes on each end of the rails to attach the post and a row of four pocket holes on the top rails (shown here) to attach the breadboard top.

measure ½ in. from each edge to mark their locations, then drill the holes. The top rails have an additional row of pocket holes to attach the breadboard top to the dresser. Mark for a hole at 2 in., 5 in., 9 in., and 12 in., and drill. Now put aside the side panels, posts, and top rails, and take out the bottom panel and lower side rails.

Prepping the Bottom Panel

The bottom panel attaches to the bottom side rails with biscuits and pocket screws. On the panel, the biscuit slots are located on the sides at 2½ in., 8 in., and 13½ in. from the front corners. On the rails, the biscuits are located at 1½ in., 7 in., and 12½ in. from the front corners. The top of the rails and the top of the panel are flush, so set them face down and use the bench as a reference fence to cut the biscuit slots. The pocket holes are located on the top side of the bottom panel. Starting at the front corners, mark ½ in., 5 in., 11 in., and 15¾ in. on both sides, and drill for the pocket holes on the top side face of the panel.

Set the bottom side rails aside. Take out the lower 32-in. front rail, and label the front and top face. The lower rail attaches to the bottom panel with pocket screws only. The lower rail attaches to the posts with a pocket screw on the

With the top of the bottom panel face down, cut the biscuits using the benchtop as a reference.

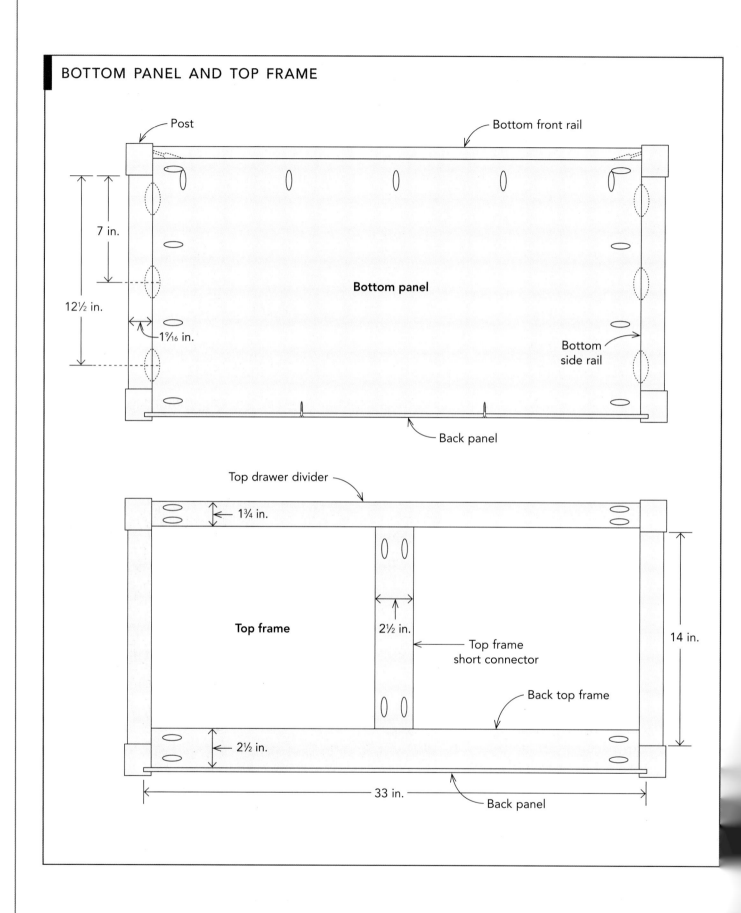

Post

Bottom front rail

7 in.

12½ in.

1⁹⁄₁₆ in.

Bottom panel

Bottom side rail

Back panel

Top drawer divider

1¾ in.

2½ in.

Top frame

2½ in.

Top frame short connector

14 in.

Back top frame

33 in.

Back panel

Center the dividers over the pocket hole bushings that are 9/16 in. apart and drill the holes.

inside face, toward the bottom edge on each end. On the inside face of the rail at each end, make a mark ½ in. up from the bottom edge and drill a pocket hole. The bottom panel has a row of pocket holes on the top face on the front edge at 2 in., 9 in., 16 in., 23 in., and 30 in. Mark and drill the pocket holes.

Prepping the Drawer Dividers

Now it's time to work on the four white oak drawer dividers. Label the dividers top, #1, #2, and #3. The top and first dividers are handled differently than #2 and #3 since there is an additional vertical drawer partition in the middle. When finish-sanding, it's important that the edges in the middle of the dividers, where the top drawer partition is located, be carefully rounded over no more than 1/16 in. Otherwise, a gap might appear under the partition, which is set back 1/16 in. from the horizontal divider face. The vertical partition front edge is flush with the drawer fronts. Make a mark or use a scrap of blue tape to remind yourself to go light on these edges.

With the right-angle jig holding the top drawer partition, use the face clamp to secure the edge-band.

Dividers #2 and #3 have a pair of pocket holes on the top side on both ends. Center the dividers on the pocket hole jig over the pair of bushings that are $\frac{9}{16}$ in. apart or make marks $\frac{1}{2}$ in. in from each side and drill the pocket holes (see the top photo on p. 163). The top divider has two pocket holes on each end on the top side. The first divider has two pocket holes on each end on the underside. Drill these pocket holes. There are also two alder drawer dividers at the back of the dresser. The top divider is $\frac{3}{4}$ in. by $2\frac{1}{2}$ in. by 32 in. and has two pocket holes on the top side on both ends $\frac{1}{2}$ in. from each side. The lower divider is $\frac{3}{4}$ in. by $1\frac{1}{2}$ in. by 32 in. and has two pocket holes on the bottom side on both ends.

The top drawer partition has a plywood core with a solid-wood edge-band. Cut a scrap of

$\frac{3}{4}$-in. plywood $5\frac{3}{4}$ in. wide at least 16 in. long. (Cut an additional piece of plywood at $5\frac{3}{4}$ in. wide around 8 in. long and label it "top drawer jig" to use later during assembly.) The edge-band must be the same thickness as the plywood, which is often a hair under $\frac{3}{4}$ in. Choose a nice piece about $1\frac{3}{4}$ in. wide with enough length to send through the planer until it's the same thickness as the plywood. On the front edge of the drawer partition, measure from both the top and bottom 2 in. and mark for the pocket holes. Cut the white oak edge-band $5\frac{3}{4}$ in., the same width as the plywood partition. Again, these must be exactly the same, otherwise a small gap could develop at the butt joint. (Having the edge-band a hair long would be preferable to having it too short.) Use the right-angle jig to

To prepare to groove the back posts for the back panel on the tablesaw, mark on the fence where the sawblade rises and lowers from the table.

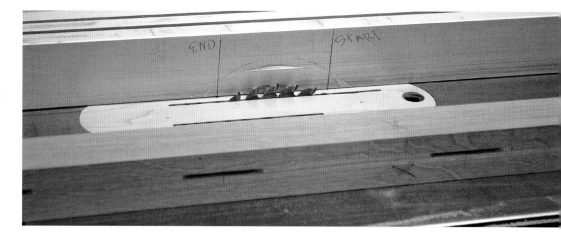

Lower the post onto the blade using the start mark on the post and the start mark on the fence as a guide.

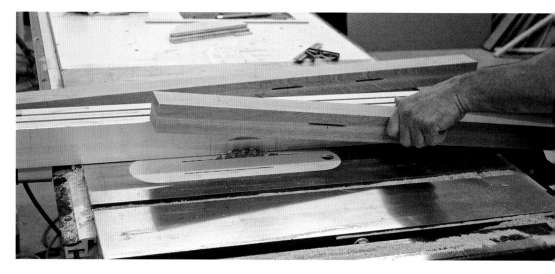

Check the fit of the groove using a small strip of plywood from the back panel stock.

help hold the partition upright and hold the edge-band to the partition with the face clamp while screwing (see the bottom photo on p. 163).

Grooving the Back Posts

The only thing left to machine on the dresser parts is the groove in the back posts for the back panel. The groove is located $5/16$ in. in from the back edge of the back posts and is around $1/4$ in. wide. The groove starts at the top of the post but stops 4 in. from the bottom. This stop cut is milled with multiple passes on the tablesaw (using a router table with a $1/4$-in. plywood bit would also work).

Clearly label the inside face where the groove is located and the back face that will be against the saw fence. The outside 2-in. face of the post will be up when cutting the groove. To know when to stop the cut, measure up from the bottom of the posts on the outside faces 4 in. and make a mark. On the right post, label the 4-in. mark "end"; on the left post, label the 4-in. mark "start." On the tablesaw, raise the blade $1/2$ in. and set the fence at $5/16$ in. Use a square to mark the location on the saw table where the blade comes up out of the table and where the blade goes back under. Transfer these marks to the saw fence so that they can be seen while ripping the groove. Label the front mark "start" and the back mark "end" (see the top photo on the facing page).

The groove in the back posts for the back panel is completely hidden from view, so the end of the groove doesn't have to be exact.

Start with the right back post. The top of the post starts the cut and the biscuit slots should be facing outward. This cut will stop 4 in. from the bottom of the post when the 4-in. start mark on the post meets the start mark on the saw fence. When the post reaches this mark, stop the cut and lift the post off the blade. The left post will start with the bottom over the blade and the 4-in. end mark on the post even with the end mark on the saw fence. Keeping the post against the fence, lower it over the moving blade and push it through the top of the post. Quarter-inch plywood usually measures less than $1/4$ in., so bump the fence over $1/16$ in. Start the cut on the back right post, then back it out and check the fit with a scrap of $1/4$-in. plywood. Continue to bump the fence over and start the cut and back it out until the scrap fit is good, then complete the cuts in the same manner as the first passes on the posts.

Getting Ready for Assembly

All the parts for the dresser carcase can now be planed, scraped, and sanded. After everything has been prepped, there are two options. One is to assemble the dresser unfinished and then build the drawers. The other is to prefinish the dresser parts and build the drawer boxes while waiting for the finish coats to dry. Both options have their merits. Assembling the dresser with prefinished parts requires special care not to ding things but makes applying finish much easier in all of the tight corners. Assembling the dresser unfinished is easier since you don't have to worry so much about the surfaces. Oiling the dresser after it is assembled is straightforward, plus the interior will not need finish. If you decide to prefinish (my preference), skip ahead to the drawer construction while you wait for parts to dry.

Assembling the Dresser Case

Assembly starts with the side panels and rails. Even though there are biscuits to keep things aligned, you still need to clamp across the joint.

When clamping the side-panel assembly, set two ¾-in.-thick cauls across the bar clamps. Place fabric on the face of each caul so that the panel doesn't get scratched.

Set the biscuits in the rails, then press them onto the panel.

Make sure the sides of the panel and the ends of the rail are flush, then drive pocket screws through the panel into the rails.

Tweaking a Rail that Is Too Long

Earlier I mentioned that cutting the rails and panels to the exact same length is a bit harder than it sounds. One of my rails must have grown overnight because when it came time to clamp it to the panel it was just a hair proud (or the panel was a hair narrow). While the gap would be minimal, it would stand out from the otherwise tight joint. I didn't feel comfortable trimming the end since it seemed like it was a microscopic amount. Using a handplane on the end grain of the rail was an option, but 2 in. by 1⁹⁄₁₆ in. of white oak end grain would be tough to plane cleanly.

Removing just a small amount of wood below the surface makes it easier to pare the rail to fit.

Using a sharp plane blade or chisel, pare the end grain of the rail so that it is flush with the panel side.

I chose instead to trim off a very small amount ³⁄₈ in. below the surface of the face of the rail (photo above). This way, if I took off too much it would be hidden. Then I used a plane blade and sanding block to flush up the ends (photo at left). The butt joint might have a gap in back, but with the massive edge joint created by the panel and all the pocket screws the joint would still be plenty strong. After the rail was trimmed, I flushed up the opposite side, drove the pocket screws through the panel into the rail, then used a plane blade to pare down the protruding end grain until it was flush with the plywood core.

With the biscuits in the slots, press the back post down onto the side-panel assembly.

Clamp across the joint, and use the face clamp and a shim to hold the post tight against the rail as you drive the pocket screws.

Set two 48-in. clamps on the bench with ¾-in.-thick cauls spanning across the bars (see the photos on p. 166). Insert the biscuits and press-fit the top and bottom rail onto the panel. Use a straightedge to make sure the sides of the panel and the ends of the rails are flush. Tighten the clamps and then drive screws through the panel into the rails, starting in the middle.

ATTACHING THE POSTS

To attach the posts, first clamp the panel/rail assembly with the back edge up to the right-angle jig. Place biscuits in the slots, and press the back post down onto the panel/rail. Making sure the top of the post and rail are flush, use a couple of clamps to hold the post in place. Then with the face clamp and a ³⁄₁₆-in. shim to account for the ³⁄₁₆-in. step, secure the bottom rail to the post. Drive two pocket screws. Repeat the procedure at the top rail-to-post joint. Finish off by screwing through the panel into the post. Unclamp and flip the assembly so the back post is on the bench. Repeat the procedure with the front post. Set the assembly aside, and start

Set the bottom panel in position so that there is a ³⁄₁₆-in. step between the front post and the rail.

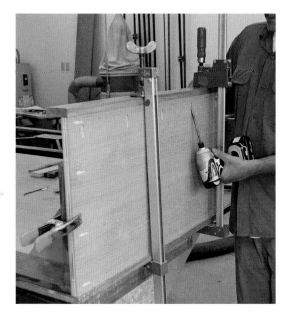

With the bottom panel clamped to the right-angle jig and the bottom front rail clamped to the bottom panel, drive pocket screws through the panel into the rail.

Position the bottom panel onto the side-panel assembly and attach with pocket screws.

again with the other panel/rail assembly with its back edge up and attach the back post. Flip the assembly and attach the front post.

ATTACHING THE FRONT RAIL

The next step is to attach the front rail to the bottom panel, but first the bottom panel needs to be ripped to its finished width. Lay a post and panel end on the bench with the inside facing up. Place a couple of biscuits in the lower rail, and set the bottom panel into place. Butt the rail against the bottom panel, and locate the rail/bottom panel so that there is a ³⁄₁₆-in. step between the front post and the rail (see the bottom photo on the facing page). At the back, mark the location of the inside of the groove for the plywood back. The bottom panel will get ripped to this mark. When the plywood back is installed, it will slide down into the groove in the back posts, past the bottom panel. Then screws are driven through the plywood back into the bottom panel to hold it in place.

On the underside of the bottom panel, there's one pocket screw that goes from the bottom rail into the front post.

Use the back top frame clamped to the right-angle jig as a spacer to support the side panel when screwing through the bottom panel into the side-panel assembly.

Clamp across the dresser at the back when screwing the back top alder frame.

Clamp across the dresser when screwing the top drawer divider to the side panels.

If the pocket hole through the back top frame lands on top of a pocket hole in the side-panel assembly, use a longer 1½-in. screw instead of the standard 1¼-in. screw.

Rip the bottom panel to width, then clamp it to the right-angle jig. Position the bottom rail so the ends are flush with the bottom panel. Clamp and drive pocket screws so that the top of the rail and panel are flush (see the top left photo on p. 169). This joint will be hidden by the drawer, so a perfect reveal is not necessary.

ASSEMBLING THE REST OF THE CASE

Lay a protective blanket on the bench, and set a side-panel assembly with the inside face up. Set the bottom panel into place with the biscuits, making sure the back meets the inside edge of the groove in the post. Drive pocket screws through the bottom panel into the bottom rail. On the underside, there's one more pocket hole through the bottom front rail into the front post (see the bottom photo on p. 169). Predrill ⅛ in. deep with the long drill bit, then drive the screw into the front post.

Next, take the 2½-in. back top frame and center it at the top of the post-and-panel assembly. Use the right-angle jig and a spring clamp to hold it upright so that the opposite post-and-panel assembly can be set into place. Locate biscuits into the bottom panel, then carefully lower the post and panel onto the bottom panel and back top frame. Make sure the back of the bottom panel is flush with the inside edge of the groove in the back post. Drive pocket screws through the bottom panel into the side rail. On the underside of the rail, again predrill ⅛ in. and drive a pocket screw through the front rail into the front post.

Set the top drawer divider at the front of the carcase, with the face of the rail ³⁄₁₆ in. back from the face of the post. Clamp it into place and drive the pocket screws. Set the alder rail at the back of the carcase on the inside edge of the groove. Flush it to the top, clamp across the joint, and drive pocket screws into the corner posts. The inside pocket hole on the back alder rail might line up exactly with the pocket hole on the post-and-panel rail. If the 1¼-in. screw

Hold the top frame short connector with a face clamp when driving the pocket screws.

Place the top drawer partition in position and mark its length.

Use spacers on either side of the top drawer partition to center it during installation.

With the 5¾-in. jig spacers on either side, set the #1 horizontal drawer divider on top with the pocket holes facing up.

does not get enough purchase, use a 1½-in. pocket screw instead.

Flip the dresser onto its back and measure the inside distance between the top rail and the back top frame. Cut a 2½-in. by ¾-in. strip of alder (the "top frame short connector" in "Materials" on p. 154) to this measurement. Drill two pocket holes on both ends. Center the connector in the cabinet, and hold with the face clamp while driving pocket screws (see the top photo on p. 171).

Setting the Drawer Dividers and Partition

Flip the dresser up onto its top, and set the top drawer partition in the cabinet. Push the front face ¹⁄₁₆ in. back from the front of the top rail. Mark the back edge where it meets the back of the back top frame (see the bottom photo on p. 171). Cut the partition to this mark. On the side of the partition without the pocket holes, mark along the top edge at ¾ in., 4 in., 12 in., and 16 in., and drill pocket holes at these locations.

With a 32-in. inside cabinet width and a ¾-in. drawer partition, the space on either side of the partition should be 15⅝ in. Cut two scraps of wood so that they fit exactly on either side of the partition and are equal in length. It should be a tight fit. Clamp the partition to the

Drive a pocket screw through a countersunk hole on the underside of the frame into the top drawer partition.

top rail and drive the front pocket screw (see the top left photo above). Flip the dresser around, place spacers on either side of the partition, and drive the back pocket screw. Drive the pocket screws in the middle, using the spacers to keep the partition from bowing.

Now locate the 5¾-in.-wide top drawer jig that you cut earlier (see p. 164). Cut the jig in half and place the two pieces against the front corner posts. Set the #1 horizontal drawer divide on top of the 5¾-in. scraps, with the face of the

With 10¼-in. spacers supporting the #3 drawer divider, drive pocket screws through the divider into the corner post.

Cut the spacers down to 8½ in. to support the #2 drawer divider.

divider set back ³⁄₁₆ in. from the front of the posts. Drive pocket screws into the posts. Slide the 5¾-in. spacers toward the back so that the posts do not get scratched.

Clamp the two 15⅝-in. spacers on either side of the top drawer partition on the lower #1 divider. From underneath, drill one hole with the pocket screw bit through the frame, countersinking it ¼ in. Drive a pocket screw through the frame into the partition.

Turn the dresser around so that the back faces out. Place the 5¾-in. drawer spacers on either end and install the back bottom frame in the same way. Make sure the back edge of the frame is flush with the inside edge of the plywood back groove.

Next, set the dresser upright so that the front is facing out, and cut two 10¼-in. scraps to help locate the #3 drawer divider. Set the rail ³⁄₁₆ in. back from the front of the post and clamp across the joint to hold it in place. Drive pocket screws at both ends, then slide the 10¼-in. spacers toward the back to remove them. Cut the 10¼-in. spacers to 8½ in. long, and repeat the drawer

A ⅝-in. alder spacer at the back of the cabinet on either side provides a screwing surface for attaching the back of the drawer slide. Drive pocket screws through the spacer into the back post.

Drawer Slides and Drawer Sides

Different brands of drawer slides usually require different drawer dimensions. I use the Tandem plus Blumotion 563F, which are specific to ¾-in. drawer sides. Tandem plus Blumotion offers a really smooth self-closing drawer slide that's concealed from view. Drawers are simple to install and remove from the slides. I like that the drawers sit on top of the slides instead of being screwed to them. There is more mechanical advantage and less reliance on screws to hold the slides in place.

Blum publishes a large booklet that covers all its models. The only change I make to the specs is to add ¹⁄₁₆ in. to the length of the drawer side. This helps the rear pin to seat more securely and also offsets any inward shift of the drawer front and backs during assembly. With a 32-in.-wide opening, the overall drawer width is 31⁹⁄₁₆ in. (subtract ⁷⁄₁₆ in. from the inside cabinet width). Subtracting 1½ in. for the drawer-side widths gives a front and back drawer part length of 30¹⁄₁₆ in. The sides are 15¹⁄₁₆ in. long. The maximum height of the drawer is ⅞ in. less than the drawer opening. Any height under that maximum will work. I usually make them 1 in. less than the opening height. On larger drawers, it's often dependent on the width of the planks I have available and whether I want to glue up boards to get the width.

Rip the drawer parts to width, then separate into drawer groups. Shown at front are the Tandem drawer slides with locking clips (and spec sheet).

divider installation using the 8½-in. spacers on top of the bottom drawer divider.

The back of the drawer slides do not reach the back post, so you need to install a pair of spacers so that the drawer slides can be screwed to the carcase (see the bottom photo on p. 173). For the spacers, use the alder strips that were used to hold the biscuit jointer up while cutting the slots into the posts. These should be the right thickness and length. Drill pocket holes measuring from the bottom at 2 in., 10 in., 20 in., and 28 in. and install the spacers at the back of the dresser, driving screws into the back posts.

Making the Drawers

The drawers on the dresser are solid wood (as opposed to the plywood drawers used on the Daybed p. 77 and Bathroom Vanity p. 120). Mill the stock to thickness first and then separate into drawer groups. The sides need to be

Use a drill press and fence to drill the index holes in the drawer backs.

Check that the groove for the drawer bottom is not too tight.

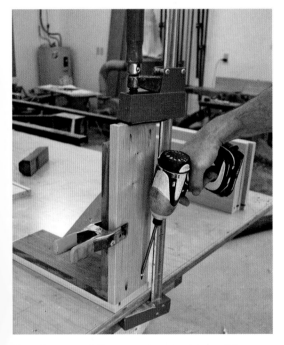

Start by assembling one drawer side and front.

Clamp across the drawer width when driving pocket screws into the drawer sides.

good on both faces; the fronts and backs need only one good face. Label the parts for each drawer. Rip the sides to 1 in. less than the height of the drawer opening. Rip the fronts to ³⁄₁₆ in. less than the drawer side height. Rip the backs to ¹⁵⁄₁₆ in. less than the drawer side height. When all the drawer parts have been ripped to width, cut them to length.

Separate out the drawer backs and drill the two ¼-in. index holes that the locating pins on the back of the drawer slides fit into. (This hole can also be drilled after the drawers are assembled.) The index holes are drilled ⁹⁄₃₂ in. over from the edge and ³⁄₁₆ in. up from the bottom edge on-center. This leaves just ¹⁄₁₆ in. wood between the bottom edge of the back and the side of the hole. On the drill press, set a ¼-in. bit to cut a hole ¹⁄₁₆ in. from the fence and around ⁷⁄₁₆ in. deep. Mark over with a scribe ⁹⁄₃₂ in. from the ends. Eyeball each hole or set stop blocks for one side, drill all the holes, then move the stop block for the other side and drill the rest of the holes.

On the drawer fronts and sides, mill the drawer bottom grooves ¼ in. wide, ½ in. up from the bottom edge and ⁵⁄₁₆ in. deep. Group fronts and backs together, and drill pocket holes on the outside faces, being careful to avoid the index holes on the drawer backs. Sand the parts, rounding over the top edges.

Start by assembling one drawer side and front (see the bottom left photo on p. 175). Align the bottom edges and attach the back to the side so that the lower edge of the back is flush with the top edge of the drawer bottom groove. Attach the other side.

Slide in the drawer bottom and pin in the center of the back. Predrill and use a pocket screw. Use a self-centering bit to attach the clips for the drawer slides at the front. Hold the clips in place with one hand, and drive the screws with the other.

FITTING THE DRAWER FRONTS

Cut the drawer fronts to fit the openings, with a finished reveal of ¹⁄₁₆ in. on all four sides. I set ¹⁄₁₆-in. shims on two sides, then compare the gap on the remaining two sides. If a ¹⁄₁₆-in. shim almost fits but not quite, then I call it ready for sanding. Check the drawer front openings with a square. If the openings are out of square, allow for more wood to custom fit.

You can use a scrap of ¼-in. MDF to check the opening width and to check for square. Cut the MDF to the measured width, set it in the opening, and slide it until it meets the corner post. If the end reveal is consistent, the opening is square. If the reveal isn't consistent, make note of where wood needs to be removed from the drawer

A scrap of MDF or other sheet material cut square at the end can help determine if the angle between the drawer divider and the post is square.

Cut and sand the drawer fronts until there is an even ¹⁄₁₆-in. reveal on all four sides.

Biscuits keep the wide center panel and breadboard ends of the top flush during seasonal shifts of the solid-wood center.

WORK
SMART

Even though the breadboard ends are held together with pocket screws and biscuits, the top is still going to move slightly. Gently rounding over the edges between the breadboard ends and the center panel will hide any movement that might occur during seasonal changes to the panel width.

front. When all the drawer fronts have been fit to the opening, drill out the backs for the drawer front locaters (see p. 180) and finish-sand/oil.

**WORK
SMART**

When fitting the drawer fronts, start at the bottom with the largest drawer opening and then cut the width of the MDF scrap as you work your way up. That way, you can use the same scrap of MDF to fit all the drawers.

Making the Breadboard Top

The dresser top is made up of a wide center panel and two short breadboard ends. Start by gluing up then cutting the center panel to ¾ in. by 19⅜ in. by 32 in. The breadboard ends are ¾ in. by 3 in. by 19¾ in. Clean up the panel and ends, getting rid of all the machine marks and sanding with 120 grit. Two pocket screws located just off of center on the panel pin it in the middle (see the drawing on p. 157). Five biscuits serve as splines to keep the two surfaces flush and allow seasonal shifts across the grain. Flip the panel so the underside is facing up. Locate the

Use the right-angle jig and face clamp to hold the dresser top in position as you drive the pocket screws into the breadboard ends.

Attach the top to the dresser before sanding it flat.

Press the drawer slide onto the drawer, and with the drawer front against the drawer box, measure the distance to the front of the slide.

center at each end. Make a mark for a pocket hole 1½ in. off-center in both directions and on both ends. The biscuit locations in the breadboard top have to avoid the pocket screws from the top rail that attach it. There is one biscuit in the center of the panel; the next two biscuits are 3½ in. from the center in both directions; the last two biscuits are 2 in. in from the front and back edges.

Butt the breadboard ends up against the panels so that there is an even ³⁄₁₆-in. overhang at the front and back. Transfer the biscuit marks from the panel to the breadboard ends. With the top

The breadboard top cannot be installed with the top outside drawer slides in place. Install them with the other drawer slides, but know that they will have to be removed to attach the top.

of the panel and ends face down on the bench, use the benchtop as a reference fence to cut the biscuit slots in the panel and ends. Drill the pocket holes in the panel. To assemble the top, clamp the panel to the right-angle jig. Set the ends on with biscuits and hold with the face clamp in place while driving the pocket screws (see the bottom photo on p. 177).

Install the top on the dresser carcase in order to sand it flat. Clamp the panel to the front and back rails, and slowly drive all four screws on each side. Sand with 120 grit until the top is flat and then finish-sand, working your way up through the grits to 220 or 320. Before removing the top from the dresser to apply oil, make some pencil marks underneath to help relocate the top for the final installation. Remove the top from the dresser, unscrew the breadboard ends, and put a slight chamfer along the edges between the ends and the center panel. Apply finish to the panel and ends before reassembling.

Installing the Drawer Slides

With the drawers built and drawer fronts fit to the opening, it's time to install the drawer slides. The slides on this dresser are set 1 in. back from

Transfer the height of the #2 divider onto a strip of plywood; this strip will be used to support the drawer slide during installation.

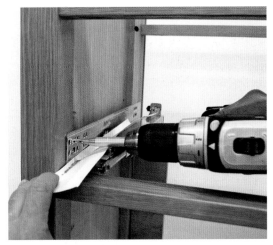

A folded strip of paper helps catch the debris from the drill when drilling for the drawer slides.

Set the drawer onto the slides to check the fit.

the horizontal drawer dividers. To come up with this measurement, install a slide onto a drawer, press the drawer front against the drawer box, and measure the distance back to the slide (see the top right photo on the facing page). Add 1/16 in. to this distance to create the step between the drawer front and the drawer partitions.

Next, make a jig to help support the drawer slide during installation. You'll need a long strip of plywood at least 21 in. long. Place it inside the cabinet up against the #2 drawer divider below the 7-in. drawer opening. Mark the top of the divider on the plywood strip and cut to the mark. On another plywood strip, mark the top of the #3 divider below the 8½-in. drawer opening and cut to the mark. Pocket-screw the two strips together, making sure that the bottoms are flush.

Start with the 7-in. drawer opening, using the jig to support the back of the slides. Set the drawer slide in the opening 1 in. back from the front face of the divider. Using a self-centering bit, drill one hole, drive a screw, and then check that the slide did not shift. Predrill and screw

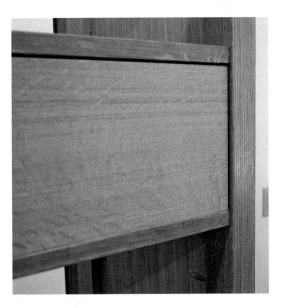

Press the drawer front against the installed drawer to check the setback reveal.

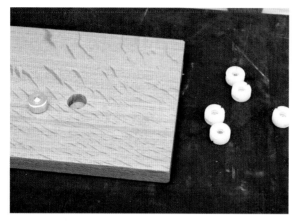

A dowel pin transfers the center of the locater hole to the drawer box.

With shims in place on the drawer divider, set the drawer front into the opening and press to transfer the center mark.

A small point locates where the 3/16-in. hole should be drilled.

Predrill and drive pocket screws through the drawer into the drawer front.

until the slide is secure. Repeat on the opposite side. Place the drawer and the drawer front in the opening to check the reveals. Work your way down the dresser, installing the slides. The top row of slides has a frame support in the back, so there's no need for a jig here.

Installing the Drawer Fronts

I apply finish to the drawer fronts first and then use dowel locaters to transfer the drill hole to the drawers. When deciding where to drill for

the locaters, take into consideration where the handles will be. A hole 3 in. down from the top of the drawer front and about 4 in. in from the end on both sides is a good location for these drawers. Set two 1/16-in. shims under the drawer front, center it in the opening, and press to transfer the mark. After the mark has been transferred, remove the dowel pins, then pound the white plastic locaters into the drawer front. Drill out the hole in the drawer box front with a 3/16-in.

bit. Use #8-32 by 1⅛-in. screws to attach the drawers to the drawer front locaters in the drawer front. Don't tighten them so much that the drawer can't be adjusted. Close the drawer and check the reveal, shift the drawer as needed, and tighten the screws in the locaters. From the inside, predrill and drive two pocket screws on each end to secure the drawer front.

Making the Drawer Handles

There are many wonderful Arts and Crafts handles available commercially, but making your own handles is a great way to customize your project. The white oak handles I made for this dresser use a hidden pocket screw in back of the bar to attach the end blocks. The challenge comes in the cleanup of the small end blocks and being careful not to split them when attaching with pocket screws. The back of the handle needs to fit flush against the drawer front, so precise assembly is necessary. I've laid out a careful step-by-step procedure to ensure an even, strong fit.

Cut the slot in the end blocks by making multiple passes over the tablesaw blade.

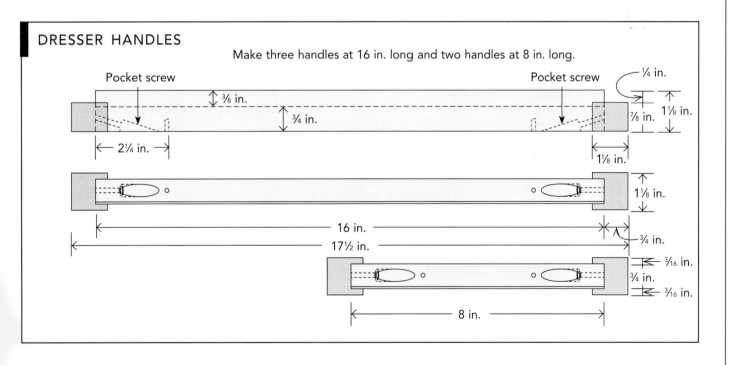

DRESSER HANDLES

Make three handles at 16 in. long and two handles at 8 in. long.

Pocket screw   Pocket screw

¼ in.

⅜ in.

¾ in.

⅞ in.   1⅛ in.

2¼ in.

1⅛ in.

1⅛ in.

16 in.

17½ in.

¾ in.

3/16 in.

¾ in.

3/16 in.

8 in.

Cutting a shallow dado on the underside of the handle bar gives a positive grip when opening the drawers.

Drill holes on the backs of the handle ⅜ in. deep to install the handles onto the drawer fronts.

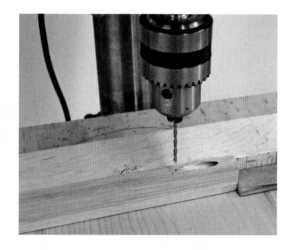

After drilling the shallow holes in the handles, drill a ⁷⁄₆₄-in. hole in the jig stock only; this hole will be used to drill out the drawer fronts.

Mill up one 1⅛-in. by 1⅛-in. by 18-in. strip for the end blocks and four ¾-in. by 1⅛-in. by 17-in. strips of the wood to be used for the handles. Also, to build the jig to drill out for the handles, mill one strip of any available species ¾ in. by 1⅛ in. by 26 in. To cut the dado in the 1⅛-in. by 1⅛-in. end block, set the tablesaw fence at ³⁄₁₆ in. and raise the sawblade ⅜ in. (A dado blade would make this go faster, but making passes with a single blade and moving the fence over is pretty quick work, too.) Make a pass over the blade with the 1⅛-in. square piece. Bump the fence over ⅛ in., and make another pass over the blade. Continue bumping the fence over ⅛ in. and making a pass over the blade until you approach an ¹¹⁄₁₆-in.-wide dado. At this point, check the fit between the ¾-in. handle strips and the dado. You want the fit to be snug since wood will be removed from the ¾-in. strips but not too tight that it will break the delicate sides of the groove.

On the horizontal handle bars, choose which ¾-in. face will be front and which 1⅛-in. face will be up; label these faces. To help give a positive grip when opening the drawer, the underside of the bar gets a lip cut into it with a single pass over the tablesaw with the blade set ¾ in. high and the fence set at ¹¹⁄₁₆ in. (see the top photo at left). The front face will be up and the up face will be against the saw fence. Do not cut the lip in the jig stock. There are three handle bars at 16 in. and two bars at 8 in. long. Cut three bars and one jig bar to 16 in. Cut the remaining 17-in. bar and jig stock so that you have two 8-in. handles and one 8-in. jig bar. On the underside of the handle stock, drill a pocket hole at both ends centered on the ¹¹⁄₁₆-in. width. Do not drill pocket holes in the jig stock. On the jig stock, label a ¾-in. face front and a 1⅛-in. face top.

Next, drill ⅛-in. holes with the drill press on the bars and jig stock, using a ⅛-in. brad-point drill bit. On the drill press, set up a fence and stop block to drill a ⅛-in. hole centered on the underside 2¼ in. from the end. With the front face down and the top face against the fence,

A pencil eraser helps to hold the small end block when crosscutting to length.

drill the ⅛-in. hole ⅜ in. deep. Just drill one hole per bar on both the handle and jig stock. Leaving the fence set, move the stop block to the opposite side of the drill bit. Set the block to drill holes 2¼ in. from the end. Drill the second hole in the handle and jig stock. Remove the stop block, but leave the fence set. Take out the ⅛-in. drill, and chuck a standard ¹¹⁄₆₄-in. bit into the drill press. Set the depth on the drill press to drill all the way through. Place the jig stock in the same manner as before with the front face down and the top against the fence, and bore out the ⅛-in. hole. Drill both the 16-in. and 8-in. jig bars with the ¹¹⁄₆₄-in. bit.

Now it's time to cut the handle end blocks on the tablesaw. Cut twelve ⅞-in.-long blocks out of the 1⅛-in. by 1⅛-in. stock (this allows for two extras, just in case). To minimize blowout, have the dado facing the blade and back up the cut with a scrap of wood. Set a stop block and use the eraser end on a pencil to hold the small block in place while cutting (as shown in the photo above). There is quite a bit of cleanup on these blocks. The end grain will be front and center, so getting rid of sawmarks is important. If the dado

Predrill the end blocks of the handle using a 15-degree gauge, shimming up the handle bar with card stock so that it is flush with the end block. Clamp across the end block and hold in place with the face clamp.

Flatten the back of the handles on a sheet of sandpaper on a machine top.

Drawer Front Drill Jig

Rip two pieces from a scrap of plywood: one 4 in. by 14 in. and one 1½ in. by 14 in. Drill four pocket holes in the 4-in. strip, two along the bottom and two along the top. **1** Clamp and attach the 4-in. plywood strip to the 16-in. handle jig that you made earlier with the top face attaching to the 4-in. scrap and the front face out. **2** The back of the jig strip and the back of the 4-in. scrap must be flush. Then to hold the jig flush with the top of the drawer front, attach the 1½-in. strip to the top of the 4-in. strip. The 1½-in. strip should overhang the back of the 4-in. plywood strip by ¾ in. **3**

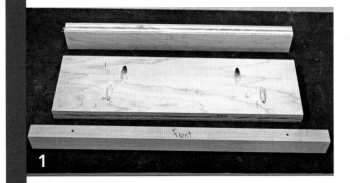

was cut with multiple passes on the tablesaw, there will be ridges that have to be pared off with a chisel or filed flat. These surfaces don't need to be perfectly flat because the bar end will be held tight with a pocket screw. Knock down all the edges on the top and sides of the blocks. Make sure the bottom edge that butts against the drawer front is crisp. Inside the dado, chamfer the edge just a hair with a file.

Clean up the handle bars, removing all the machine marks. Check how the ends of the bars fit in the blocks; the fit cannot be too tight, or the delicate sides of the dado will break. Before finishing with oil, assemble the handles. Group the handles into pairs and label them so that each bar end has a specific block. The step between the bar and block is ¼ in., but there was sanding and planing on both parts, so this step will vary between handles. Use ¼-in. scrap and some strips from card stock. Set the block on the ¼-in. scrap. Set the card stock shims under the bar until the surfaces are flush, then use the face clamp to hold them together. To improve your chances of not splitting the block when drilling, clamp across the block. Predrilling with the long bit is also helpful. To keep the bit at the desired 15-degree angle, I cut a small block as a gauge (see the center photo on p. 183). Drill roughly ¼ in. deep, then drive the pocket screw. Using this procedure on white oak with fine-threaded 1¼-in. pocket screws, I did not have a single blowout. With the handles assembled, check that they sit flush against the drawer front. Laying sandpaper on a machine surface and moving the assembled handle back and forth will clean up any high spots.

You can finish the handles assembled or take them apart and finish them. I choose to disassemble them to finish and found that reassembling them with all the parts labeled was easy work.

ATTACHING THE HANDLES

To drill the drawer fronts for the handles, you'll need to make a jig (see the sidebar on the facing page). Set the jig on the bottom drawer. The end

Attach the drawer jig to the drawer with the face clamp, then drill out for the handles.

After the holes are drilled, attach the handle.

of the 16-in. handle jig should be $7.^{15}\!/_{16}$ in. over from the end of the drawer front. Holding the jig in place with the face clamp, drill two $^{11}\!/_{64}$-in. holes all the way through the drawer front and drawer box (see the top photo on p. 185). Attach the handle to the drawer with two 2-in. coarse-thread pocket screws. Use a screwdriver to avoid stripping out the hole.

Next, disassemble the drawer jig so that the center of the jig can be cut to drill the narrower width of drawer #3. Set the saw fence at $3\!/_{2}$ in., and rip off $\!/_{2}$ in. from the top of the 4-in. strip. You'll need to drill new pocket holes on the top edge, but the bottom pocket holes can still be used to attach the jig strip. Reassemble the jig and drill the holes for the $8\!/_{2}$-in. drawer, centering the jig on the drawer front, $7^{15}\!/_{16}$ in. from the edge. Install the handle. Disassemble the jig again, rip the center plywood strip to $2^{3}\!/_{4}$ in.

Slide the back down into the grooves in the posts until the top edge is flush with the top of the back rail.

Drive screws along the top and bottom edge to hold the back panel in place.

wide, and reassemble. Holding the jig to the 7-in. drawer front with the face clamp, drill two $^{11}/_{64}$-in. holes. Remove the jig and disassemble one last time. Rip the center plywood strip to 2¼ in. wide. This time, you'll need to attach the shorter 8-in. handle jig to the plywood strip, and you'll need to drill new pocket holes for the shorter jig. Reassemble the jig and attach to either top drawer. Center the 8-in. handle jig on the drawer front and hold with the face clamp. Drill with a $^{11}/_{64}$-in. bit.

Installing the Back

The ¼-in. back panel, which is 35¼ in. tall and 33 in. wide, has to be installed before the top. Slide the back down into the grooves until the top edge is flush with the top of the back rail. It should stay in place, but if the grooves are a bit loose, hold the back panel by clamping it to the back top frame. Predrill, then drive two pocket screws on the top and bottom edge to hold the back panel in place.

For best access, remove all the drawers and the top outer drawer slides. Install the top, then reinstall the drawer slides. Now you can fill the dresser with all those old T-shirts that you cannot bear to throw away!

To secure the top, you can add additional screws through the top center frame above the top drawer partition, but drive these screws in the center of the frame only to allow for wood movement of the center top panel.

Drive pocket screws through the top rails on the side panels into the breadboard ends.

Metric Equivalents

INCHES	CENTIMETERS	MILLIMETERS	INCHES	CENTIMETERS	MILLIMETERS
1/8	0.3	3	13	33.0	330
1/4	0.6	6	14	35.6	356
3/8	1.0	10	15	38.1	381
1/2	1.3	13	16	40.6	406
5/8	1.6	16	17	43.2	432
3/4	1.9	19	18	45.7	457
7/8	2.2	22	19	48.3	483
1	2.5	25	20	50.8	508
1 1/4	3.2	32	21	53.3	533
1 1/2	3.8	38	22	55.9	559
1 3/4	4.4	44	23	58.4	584
2	5.1	51	24	61	610
2 1/2	6.4	64	25	63.5	635
3	7.6	76	26	66.0	660
3 1/2	8.9	89	27	68.6	686
4	10.2	102	28	71.7	717
4 1/2	11.4	114	29	73.7	737
5	12.7	127	30	76.2	762
6	15.2	152	31	78.7	787
7	17.8	178	32	81.3	813
8	20.3	203	33	83.8	838
9	22.9	229	34	86.4	864
10	25.4	254	35	88.9	889
11	27.9	279	36	91.4	914
12	30.5	305			